The Mystical Mount Kailash

All You Wanted to Know:
The Legend and the Pilgrimage of
Mount Kailash and Lake Manasarovar

K RAVINDRAN

INDIA · SINGAPORE · MALAYSIA

ISBN 979-8-89233-601-7

Contents

Foreword..7

Preface...9

Acknowledgement 11

Chapter 1   Introduction 13

Chapter 2   Geographical Context............................ 15
              Mount Kailash.................................... 15
              Lakes Manasarovar and Rakshas Tal...... 19

Chapter 3   Geological Context 23

Chapter 4   Mystical and Mysterious Context.............. 25
              Abode of Mysteries and Myriad
              Secrets 26
              Strange and Curious Facts..................... 29

Chapter 5   Axis Mundi Context 37
              Where Heaven and Earth Meet............. 37
              Mount Kailash as Axis Mundi 38
              Jerusalem as Axis Mundi...................... 40
              Nature as Axis Mundi 41
              Angkor Wat as Mount Meru and
              Axis Mundi 42
              Angkor Wat as Buddhist Mandala......... 43
              Plants and Trees as Axis Mundi 44
              Humans as Axis Mundi.......................... 45

Chapter 6   Religious Context 47
              Hinduism 47

          Buddhism 48
          Jainism.. 49
          Bon religion... 49

Chapter 7   Historical Context of
                Kailash-Manasarovar 51

Chapter 8   Pilgrimage or Yatra: Kailash –
                Manasarovar: When and How?...................55

Chapter 9   Pilgrimage: Lake Manasarovar................... 57

Chapter 10   Pilgrimage: Mount Kailash: Parikrama
                or Kora.. 63
          Outer Kora 65
          Inner Kora 69
          Monasteries around Mount Kaiiash 70
          Holy spots on the Kora 72
          Nandi Parvat 76
          Ashtapada.. 76
          Gauri Kund/Parvati Sarovar................... 77

Chapter 11   Mountaineering 79

Chapter 12   Routes to Kailash-Manasarovar 81
          Season for Pilgrimage............................ 81
          Modern/Present Day Pilgrimage with
          Tibet under Chinese Control 81
          Climate change...................................... 82
          Road conditions in Tibet........................ 83
          Road Links to Kailash-Manasarovar 84
          Routes through Nepal 87
          Routes through Tibet 88
          Kailash-Manasarovar by Road Itinerary.... 88

Kailash – Manasarovar By Train............. 90
Kailash – Manasarovar By Air............... 90

Chapter 13   Panch Kailash 93
Adi Kailash..................................... 93
Shikhar Kailash (Shrikhand Mahadev
Kailash) 95
Kinnaur Kailash.................................. 98
Religious Significance 98
Kinnaur Kailash Parikrama 99
Manimahesh Kailash........................... 100
Legends 101
Pilgrimage/Trekking Season 102
Mountaineering................................... 104

Chapter 14   Conclusion................................... 105

Glossary...107
Bibliography 117
Index...119

Phone : 0265-2356426 / 63534 20198
E-mail : rkmvmvl@gmail.com
Website : www.rkmvadodara.org

Ramakrishna Mission
Vivekananda Memorial
Opp. Circuit House, R.C. Dutt Road
Alkapuri, VADODARA - 390007

Foreword

I have pleasure in writing the "Foreword" to this book of Mr K Ravindran, who is known to me for the past few years. I have scanned through the manuscript of his proposed book on "Mount Kailash and Lake Manasarovar". These sacred pilgrimage sites are visited by followers of Hinduism, Buddhism and Jainism for centuries, owing to their religious significance. This is despite the inhospitable terrain, conveyance constraints, extreme cold conditions and severely limited facilities available, during the pilgrimage period of two to three weeks.

Many of the pilgrims and trekkers have been writing about their experience in a travelogue form. The approach by Mr Ravindran in this book has been from a multidimensional viewpoint, covering not only the geographical and religious contexts, but also from a historical, geological, axis mundi, mystical and mystery backgrounds, as well. He has also given the various itineraries by the multiple routes. This is sure to enhance the usefulness of the book from the viewpoint of prospective pilgrims and trekkers.

I wish all success to this endeavour of Mr Ravindran.

Date: Vadodara
Place: 17/12/2023

– (Swami Ishtamayananda)
Secretary Ramakrishna Mission
Vivekananda Memorial, Vadodara

Preface

In May 2010, I and my wife, had undertaken the Kailash-Manasarovar pilgrimage through a private travel agency. After reaching Kathmandu by air, we took another flight to Lhasa and then by land route, we reached Lake Manasarovar. After the holy dip and driving around the beautiful lake, followed the circumambulation of Mount Kailash. The return journey was performed by the land route to Kathmandu. It was a unique experience of a lifetime and the memories are still quite fresh. However, it never occurred to me to chronicle the experience in the form of a travelogue or book.

After publication of four books between 2015 and 2022, I decided to publish in a book form, the mystique surrounding Mount Kailash and details of the arduous trek through high altitude in this most inhospitable terrain. Though source material on the subject matter is abundantly available in the present "Ask Google" age, the same remains scattered in the websites under various heads with an overload of information. The most difficult task is to select the requisite material, eschewing the chaff and non-essential, keeping in mind the target group of readers, which requires research and diligent hard work.

During the preparation of this book, I have described quite a few unique features of Mount Kailash regarding its geographical, geological, mystical, religious, historical and axis mundi contexts. I have included quite a good number of images of the trek, important spots on the trekking route and the approach routes at the appropriate contexts to enable the readers for a better appreciation. I have also dealt with, in some details, the numerous routes to Kailash, from which a prospective trekker/pilgrim can choose from, based on his/her special requirements and interests.

For the inquisitive readers, a small section at the end of the book gives brief details of the other four Kailash peaks, which are all in India in Uttarakhand and Himachal Pradesh states. These four, along with the Kailash peak in Tibet, are collectively known as "Panch Kailashas".

Since the material available from various travel agencies are in the form of brochures and itineraries, mainly from the publicity angle, a comprehensive handbook-cum-ready reckoner book of the "Lonely Planet" type is desirable for a prospective trekker/pilgrim. It is fervently hoped that this humble effort of mine would serve that purpose.

– Wg Cdr K Ravindran (Retd)
e-mail ID: ravi7931@gmail.com

Acknowledgement

This book is a result of the prodding of my two sons, Rohit and Rahul, both based abroad, to chronicle my experience of the unique pilgrimage trip I had undertaken to Lake Manasarovar and Mount Kailash many years ago, for the benefit of those who are desirous to venture on this. I must acknowledge the contribution of Rahul for his help in sequencing the Glossary and Index, during the compilation of this book.

I am grateful to revered Swami Ishtamayanandaji, Secretary of Ramakrishna Mission Vivekananda Memorial, Vadodara Centre for graciously agreeing to write the "Foreword" to the book.

Last, but not the least, I acknowledge my sincere gratitude to Notion Press, Chennai for the prompt publishing of this book.

Vadodara India

Wg Cdr K Ravindran (Retd)
Dated: 18/12/2023

CHAPTER 1

Introduction

Mount Kailash is a striking peak in the remote south-west corner of Tibet region in the Himalayan Mountains. Tibet falls within Pamirs plateau, long considered as "Roof of the world". This wonderful, breath-taking, diamond-shaped mountain is made up of black rock and is surrounded by beautiful landscape which is rugged and dry. It is one of the highest parts of Himalayas and serves as a source of some of the longest rivers in Asia.

Mount Kailash is also known as one of the most sacred mountains and is an important pilgrimage destination for four faiths: Hindus, Buddhists, Jains and the ancient Tibetan Bonpos.

In the Hindu religion, Lord Shiva is believed to reside at Mount Kailash, as it is the holy centre of the planet and a manifestation of heaven. The Buddhists believe that Mount Kailash is the abode of Buddha Demchok, who represents supreme bliss. They also believe that Kailash – Manasarovar is a symbol of harmony. According to Jainism, Mount Kailash, also recognised as Mount Ashtapada, is the site where the founder of their religion, Rishabhanatha, attained 'Nirvana' or liberation. Finally, according to the Bon religion of Tibet, Mount Kailash is regarded to be a foundation of spiritual power.

Lake Manasarovar is one of the highest fresh water lakes in the world, with its pure, immaculate and blue water. It is believed that the turquoise lake was first formed in the mind of Lord Brahma where, later, Lord Shiva and Lord Brahma appeared as swans. The holy water of Lake Manasarovar is said to have the power of washing away the sins of humans and hence a holy dip in the ice-cold water is a must for the pilgrims. Circumambulation of Mount Kailash is believed to expunge or wash away the sins of one's Karmic deeds and therefore it is undertaken by pilgrims of all the four religions.

CHAPTER 2

Geographical Context

Mount Kailash

Mount Kailash is at an altitude of around 6700 metres (22,000 ft) above mean sea level. It is located in Burang county of Ngari prefecture in the South Western part of Tibet, which is an autonomous region of China. The mount is located 2,000 kms west of Lhasa, capital of Tibet and is to the east of Garhwal and Kumaon regions of Uttarakhand state in India. Mount Kailash is less than 100 km (62 miles) north of the western tri-junction of the borders of China/ Tibet, India, and Nepal at Lipu Lekh Pass.

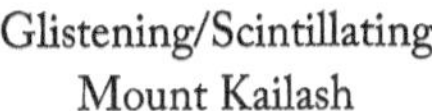

Glistening/Scintillating Mount Kailash

Another View of Mount Kailash

Mount Kailash is considered to be supremely sacred as the earthly manifestation of the Hindu mythical Mount Meru, or Sumeru. 'Meru' in Sanskrit means 'spine' or 'axis'. It is also translated as 'navel' and is also the central bead of a 'Mala' or rosary. When the approbatory prefix of 'Su' (meaning excellent, wonderful, auspicious or sacred in Sanskrit) is added, it becomes excellent, wonderful, auspicious or sacred Meru. Mount Meru is also known as Sumeru, Sineru or Mahameru. It is believed to be the spiritual centre of the universe in Hindu, Buddhist and Jain cosmology. Bon is an indigenous religion which predates Buddhism, which came to Tibet in the 7th century CE. The followers of Bon religion are known as Bonpos. Bon texts have many names for the mount such as Water's Flower, Mountain of Sea Water, Nine Stacked Swastika Mountain etc. The Axis Mundi, the centre of the universe, the navel of the world, the world pillar, Mount Meru (or Sumeru), Swastika Mountain, Mount Ashtapada, Gang Tise or Gang Rinpoche or Kang Rinpoche in Tibetan (meaning "Precious jewel of snow"), Mount Kangrinboqe – all these names, real or legendary, are bestowed upon this mount.

Mount Kailash   Mount Kailash sunset

Mountains, the most dramatic feature of the Earth, are considered by many religions as the mystical realms of the Divine, heaven, sages and spirits. Mount Kailash lies deep in the womb of eight valleys, forming an eight petalled lotus. Often referred to as the "Olympus Central Asia",

Mount Kailash denotes the axis of the world or the stairway to heaven. On the southern face of the holy mountain, a vertical gash crosses horizontal layers, resulting in the creation of the image of a Swastika. The word has its roots in Swastika, Sanskrit for well-being and good fortune. Buddhists consider the mountain to be a Mandala – the sacred circle from which the holy rivers – Indus, Satluj or Sutlej, Brahmaputra and Karnali flow, depicting the spokes of the eternal wheel. With its four façades facing the four cardinal directions, i.e. north, east, south, and west, the shape is remarkable and has led to speculations over the centuries.

Mount Kailash Swastika View

According to Vishnu Purana the mountain's four faces are made of crystal, ruby, gold, and sapphire. It is a pillar of the world and is located at the heart of six mountain ranges symbolizing a lotus. The four rivers flowing from Kailash thereon flow to the four quarters of the world and divide the world into four regions. The largest and most important rock-cut temple, Kailash Temple at Ellora, Maharashtra is named after Mount Kailash.

The Four Faces of Mount Kailash

As per Tibetan legend, the four faces of Kailash are sapphire at south (peacock), ruby at west (elephant), gold at north (lion) and crystal at east (horse), the animals representing the origins of four rivers through their mouths. River Karnali (also called Ghaghara) originates from south and becomes a tributary of Ganga (Ganges). River Sutlej/Satluj (also called Shatadru) originates from west and flows into Himachal Pradesh and later joins Indus. River Indus (also called Sindhu) originates from north and flows to Pakistan through Ladakh. River Brahmaputra (also called Yarlung Tsangpo in upper Tibet) originates from east and flows into Arunachal Pradesh (where it is joined by Lohit River) and Assam and into Bangladesh (where it is called Jamuna). It can thus be seen that four major rivers originate from around Kailash and flow into the Indian subcontinent and discharge into Arabian Sea and Bay of Bengal.

Lakes Manasarovar and Rakshas Tal

Maps of the region

The Manasarovar Lake lies at 4590 m (15,060 ft) above mean sea level, a relatively high elevation for a large freshwater lake on the mostly saline lake-studded Tibetan Plateau. It freezes in the winter. According to Brockman, it is one of the highest freshwater lakes in Asia (with the highest being Tilicho Lake in Nepal at an altitude of 4919 m).

At the base of Mount Kailash, to the south lie two lakes – Manasarovar and Rakshas Tal. The higher lake, Manasarovar, is round like the sun, and the lower lake, Rakshas Tal, resembles the shape of the crescent moon, thereby representing the solar and lunar forces respectively. Man/ Mana/Manas means 'Mind', Sarovar means 'Large lake', 'Rakshas' means 'Demon' and Tal means 'Lake' in Sanskrit. Thus, the round lake represents the inner consciousness of humans ie, the higher, spiritual desires (solar or positive forces) and the crescent lake represents the lower, base desires (lunar or dark forces).

Yaks on shore of Lake Manasarovar with Mount Kailash in the background

Satellite view of Manasarovar and Rakshas Tal

As per Hindu mythology, Ganges (Ganga) originated from the toe of Lord Vishnu, entered lunar circle, descended on the peak of Kailash where Lord Shiva's matted hair locks quelled the fury of Ganga, descended from Kailash, circum-ambulated Kailash seven times and divided into four major rivers of the Indian subcontinent as above. Again, according to Hindu mythology, Kailash was Mount Meru and Manasarovar was the ocean which was churned by Devas and Asuras, producing myriad items such as Airawat, Kamadhenu, Kalpavruksha etc and ultimately the Amrut Kalash (pot of nectar). Near Manasarovar is Lake Rakshas Tal (also called Bhairav Kund or Ravan Kund) where the Asuras had bathed and hence not used by pilgrims for bath/dip. There is a natural channel connection between Manasarovar and Rakshas Tal. Manasarovar is considered to be the lake where the Devatas and Apsaras have their bath and hence considered to be very holy where a dip by the pilgrims is believed to wash off their sins.

CHAPTER 3

Geological Context

Tibet has extensive fault lines with rocks and sediments hiding the identity of the area, Tethys Sea. The region around Mount Kailash and the Indus headwaters area is typified by wide-scale faulting of metamorphosed late-Cretaceous to mid-Cenozoic sedimentary rocks which have been intruded by igneous Cenozoic granitic rocks. Mount Kailash appears to be a metasedimentary roof pendant supported by a massive granite base. The Cenozoic rocks represent offshore marine limestones deposited before subduction of the Tethys oceanic crust. These sediments were deposited on the southern margin of the Asia block during subduction of the Tethys oceanic crust before the collision of the two tectonic plates, Indian and Eurasian. As the Indian subcontinent subducted due to this collision, Tethys Sea was lifted into the air, creating the world's largest mountain ranges in the Pamirs region, namely Himalayas, Karakoram, Hindu Kush, Tian Shan and Kunlun. The Himalayan ranges are still forming, growing taller by a few mms every year, under the continuing rubbing action of these two tectonic plates. Sea shells within the sandstones in Tibetan region are reminders of this cataclysmic event, which is said to have taken place some 5.5 million years ago when Caspian Sea became landlocked between Europe and Asia. Caspian Sea has the world's largest enclosed body of saline water. Manasarovar Lake at altitude of 4530 m, which also got formed at the same time in the Pamirs plateau, is the world's second highest body of fresh water. Another reminder of this dramatic event is the presence of thousands of sea gulls flying around Manasarovar Lake. Sea gulls are normally to be found near sea shores in other parts of the world. It is obvious that the sea gulls, though initially disoriented due to this sudden cataclysmic event, had to eventually adapt themselves to this fresh water lake with its abundant supply of a variety of fishes.

CHAPTER 4

Mystical and Mysterious Context

Mystical things or aspects are those concerning the truth beyond human understanding; of transcendental state; related to God, dealing with inscrutable spiritual power beyond the ken of human beings. Mystic and mystical are adjectives referring to the hidden spiritual power, whereas myth is a traditional narrative. Such traditional narratives usually include supernatural characters with supernatural powers. The narrators have visualised the characters and themes with their sheer imagination. The mythical narratives could also embody popular ideas of the socio-political phenomenon, imbued with imagination. Myth has another distinct meaning, as a noun. It refers to widely held popular notions, which in truth are fake notions, something that is fictitious.

Mount Kailash is Shiva's abode, that doesn't mean that Shiva is present in physical form only in Kailash, and hiding somewhere behind the snow-clad mountains. Shiva is an Energy, so He is present in every element of His creation. There is no place where Shiva doesn't exist.

Abode of Mysteries and Myriad Secrets

Mount Kailash: Swastika View

The numerous mysteries and myriad facts that are enveloped around the Kailash peak add to the grandeur of the mount. It is claimed that, many times, seven different types of light have been shining in the sky on Mount Kailash. NASA scientists believe that it may be due to the magnetic force here. According to these scientists, the magnetic force here can meet the sky and sometimes create such things. The mount is perpetually surrounded under thick silver clouds. It is said – "Universe is under no obligation to make sense to humans." Sometimes, we have to believe in the unbelievable; that is when we surrender to the supreme being. Mount Kailash is one such place on earth that has been universally accepted as divine for many reasons.

The very shape of the mountain, with four well-defined faces, facing the four cardinal directions, has been a subject of speculation for many centuries. Scientists who have studied its topography and structure claim that it has a pyramidal shape and is strictly oriented to the cardinal points. One of the theories that the Russians have put forth is that Mount Kailash could be a vast, human-built pyramid, the heart of an entire complex of a hundred smaller pyramids. Additionally, this complex might be the centre of a world-wide system connecting other monuments or sites where miraculous and paranormal phenomena have been observed. Numerous travellers, especially in the beginning of the 20th century, have come to proclaim this owing to the fact that Mount Kailash is too perfect to be a totally natural phenomenon, or at any rate it gives the appearance of human intervention. Its shape resembles a vast cathedral; the sides of the mountain are surprisingly perpendicular with a sheer fall of hundreds of metres. The strata are horizontal with the layers of stone slightly varying in colour. The dividing lines show up clear and distinct, which gives the entire mountain the facade of huge blocks of reddish stone, having been built by giant hands. If true, it could radically alter our knowledge on the growth of humanity and civilizations, necessitating the re-writing of human history.

Another secret related to Mount Kailash pertains to the rapid aging of those who are near it. Taking into consideration, for example, the growth of hair and nails, it can be appropriately assumed that 12 hours spent near Kailash is equal to two weeks in normal conditions !

The Pamir plateau has long been considered to be the "roof of the world". Mount Kailash in the Pamir plateau is thus considered the 7th chakra or crown chakra of the world. Just as the crown chakra of a human is the centre of spirituality/pure consciousness/enlightenment/bliss and connects to the divine part, Mount Kailash connects the earth to its spiritual aspect. The Hindu scriptures state that Adhya Shakti or Prakriti, the negative energy of a human, resides in the 1st chakra or Muladhara, at the base of the spine, and Shiva Shakti or Purusha, the positive energy, resides at the 7th chakra, Sahasrara. With intense practice of Yoga over a long period of time, the negative energy from the base travels upward and unites with the positive energy at the crown of the head, when knower, knowledge and the object of knowledge become one, resulting in enlightenment or bliss.

Due to the divinity bestowed on the sacred mount, it is forbidden to scale the peak of this mountain. Despite numerous attempts, no one climber has succeeded in conquering the summit of Mount Kailash. Those who approach too close to it with a wish to climb to the top of it, all of a sudden get set to go in the opposite direction. Climbing the home of the Gods and hindering with their peace and calm with mortal interferences, is considered sacrilege and a slight to immortals, and results in misfortune and death.

The most mysterious Kailash secret relates to the fact that it is adjacent to the sarcophagus Nanda. After the conduction of a number of studies, the researchers found the presence of many cavities inside the sarcophagus. Ancient Chinese legends convey that the sarcophagus serves as a refuge in which all great teachers – Krishna, Buddha, Jesus, Confucius, Zoroaster, and other sages – sent to the world for its existence, are in a "preserved" state of deep meditation (Somati or Samadhi). Their centuries-long stay is aimed at the preservation and restoration of the human gene pool in the incident of the death of civilization.

This place is one of vital importance. It is believed that when the ice finally melts, it will reveal "THE EYE". The Russian Doctor and explorer, Prof. Ernst Muldashev, Ph D, after exploring Tibet, said: "There are two underground countries, the Shambhala and Agartha, which are each part of the gene pool of humanity and civilization. Information provided by the Thule Society of Germany (Eckhart and Haushofer), shows there is a higher civilization, coming from the Gobi, from the Himalayas and divided into two branches, the Shambhala and Agartha. The former, being the centre of power, is protected by unknown forces and energy. One can assume that these places are the technogenic civilization and gene pool of humanity. It seems that not only are there underground centres in Tibet and the Himalayas, but these tunnels are widespread all over the entire globe".

Strange and Curious Facts

The following strange and curious facts about Mount Kailash will flabbergast any one:

1.Significance of Mount Kailash in different religions

Considered sanctum sanctorum of Hindus, Tibetan Buddhists, Jains and Bon religions, Mount Kailash is revered by all.

As per Hinduism, Lord Shiva, the destroyer of evil and sorrow, resides at the summit of the legendary Mount Kailash, where he sits in a state of perpetual meditation and bliss, along with his consort Parvati. It is a place where eternity meshes with time and the slightness and impermanence of mortality greet the intricacies of immortality.

The Tibetan Buddhists are of the belief that Mount Kailash is the abode of the Buddha Demchok who represents supreme bliss. It is also said that it was on this sacred mountain that Buddhism replaced Bon as the primary religion of Tibet

In Jainism, Kailash is called Mount Ashtapada and is the site where the first Jain Tirthankara, Rishabhadeva, attained liberation from rebirth.

The Bonpos maintain that the whole of the mystical region and the nine-stacked Swastika Mountain are the seat of all spiritual powers. It denotes the place where their founder, Tonpa Shenrab, descended to the earth from the sky. This mountain is also said to be the gathering place of masses of gods, among which are the highest gods of Hinduism.

Unfortunately, the citizens of India today have given in to the impact of modern civilization and world culture and many, especially in the large cities tend to de-emphasize their cultural and religious heritage, as mere superstition. This unfortunate trend has made for a clash between material and spiritual values; but the momentum of spiritual renewal continues to build and eventually the higher values will be restored in India as in the rest of the world.

The ancient 'Gods' favoured high-rise places and built installations. Ezekiel was brought to see one of these places. Zeus lived on one. So, what about Mount Kailash? Does it represent another node in a global grid, built with some out-worldly and divine technology that we cannot actually see and do not yet understand? Is it the origin of civilization? Is it suggestive of presence of nuclear activity? Can it provide us with the basis, origin and reason of our very existence and that of the entire universe?

The answers to these questions will remain embedded in the heart of the Himalayas and the mysteries of Mount Kailash will continue to intrigue millions in the future as well. One can only hope to decipher the baffling and inexplicable cryptic intricacies of Kailash. In the meanwhile, the cultural and spiritual significance of Mount Kailash which exists and will continue its existence, contrary to mortal belief, should be upheld by human civilization.

The Hindu holy scripture Bhagavad Gita states –

"Before creation I alone was, there was no other existence of the nature of cause and effect different from Me. After the creative cycle ends also, I alone exist. For, this universe is also Myself, and when everything is dissolved in its cause in Pralaya, what remains is only Myself."

No matter how different religions find their spiritual connection with Mount Kailash, the core essence is that the precious snow mountain is universally accepted as DIVINE.

2. Discovery as the centre of the world

Finding mention in the Vedas and the epic Ramayana, Mount Kailash has been scientifically discovered as the axis mundi. Various studies have proven that the quintessential divine peak is the centre of the world and is connected to significant monuments around the globe. The historic landmark of Stonehenge in England is 6666 kms away from here. The same distance holds good with the North Pole which is also 6666 kms from the mount. The distance exactly doubles with the South Pole, which is 1332 kms from Mount Kailash. These research findings have thus confirmed that Mount Kailash is the axis of rotation of the celestial sphere.

3. No human could ever climb to the peak

Many daring mountaineers have attempted to make their way to the peak of Mount Kailash, but no one could ever make it to the abode of Lord Shiva. The mountain is considered unconquered. It is advised not to climb the mountain, since that would be sacrilege and harbinger of misfortune. According to the Hindu scriptures, trespassing or meddling with the divinity of the sacred mount is a forbidden act as this can disturb the spiritual and divine energies in the region, where the Godhead, Lord Shiva, resides at the peak with his consort Parvati and his mount/vehicle Nandi. With the record of unsuccessful attempts to reach the summit, Mount Kailash remains unexplored till date. Rough weather, altitude sickness, diverging in the wrong direction and misleading trails are some of the hindrances that deter even the toughest trekkers. However, according to Buddhist scriptures, the philosopher-saint-monk Milarepa (1052-1135 CE), the champion of Vajrayana Buddhism in Tibet, could scale up the peak in the 11th century CE by riding on sun's rays. He had acquired mystical and supernatural powers under masters of his time, through practice of black magic and intense meditation respectively. He had attained God-realization and is considered the Tibetan Buddha.

4. A stairway between heaven and earth

It is mentioned in the Vedas that Mount Kailash is a stairway between heaven and earth. The four slopes of the pyramid-shaped mount face the four directions of the compass, which makes it the epitome of perfection. The Hindus therefore firmly believe that it is the gateway to heaven. According to the epic Mahabharata, after a long reign of their kingdom, the Pandavas and Draupadi left for Mount Kailash to attain Moksha. On their way, one by one, everyone slipped and fell while climbing the cliff and only the righteous and virtuous King Yudhishthira could reach heaven and was admitted.

5. Creation of OM symbol

OM Symbol on Mount Kailash

Lord Shiva, the destroyer and creator of the world resides on Mount Kailash. The symbol of OM (ॐ) formed naturally with the deposition of snow on the granite mountain is believed to be the embodiment of his presence. We live in a world of apostles and atheists. Freethinkers have their own reasons for taking it as mere coincidence, but in the heart of devotees and believers the miraculous impression of OM has an immense symbolic value. For them, it is God's creation that calls only for belief and surrender.

6. Taking a leap into time

Another astounding fact is time-travelling which suggests that the air in the mountain renders to the rapid ageing process. This transtemporal travel claim is backed by a story of climbers from Siberia. After trespassing the forbidden line, the group of climbers experienced ageing by a few decades. All these climbers died within a year's time due to the leap of age. This in itself raises curiosity and leaves us in bewilderment. Also, trekkers and pilgrims who visit Mount Kailash say that they have noted a rapid growth of their nails and hair while trekking and even after returning from the holy mountain. Whether people believe this or not, the gospel truth can be witnessed in the growth that happens in hours at Kailash as compared to the growth in a week elsewhere. This is time-travelling indeed !

7. The uncanny resemblance of the lakes with sun and moon

The two holy pristine lakes, Manasarovar and Rakshas Tal, are located at the foot of Mount Kailash. In these, one can witness the extraordinary creation of God. Manasarovar is the highest fresh water lake in the world and holds deep spiritual value owing to its crystal clear ice-cold holy water and shape that resembles the sun. Rakshas Tal is believed to have emerged out of Ravana's intense austerities to please Lord Shiva and is endowed with salty water and resembles the crescent moon. The two lakes thus personify the light and dark, the positive and negative energies that envelop the earth. Every year, many devotees go on pilgrimage to Manasarovar with full faith and belief that they would be released from sins and be cured from diseases after their holy dip in Manasarovar. While returning, they carry the holy water of the lake in a pot/pitcher/bottle, which remains pure for many years.

8. The pyramid-shaped mount looks unnatural

For centuries, the pyramid-shaped mount has captivated many scientists for research on the mystifying secrets wrapped around like a thick layer of snow. One theory by the Russian scientists suggests that Mount Kailash is way too perfect in terms of symmetry, shape and size that it is inconceivable to have occurred in the natural process of evolution. The other scientists say that the mount has striking similarities with the pyramids of Egypt or a cathedral.

CHAPTER 5

Axis Mundi Context

Where Heaven and Earth Meet

In astronomy, axis mundi is the Latin term for the axis of Earth between the celestial poles. In a geocentric coordinate system, this is the axis of rotation of the celestial sphere. Consequently, in ancient Greco-Roman astronomy, the axis mundi is the axis of rotation of the planetary spheres within the classical geocentric model of the cosmos.

In 20th-century comparative mythology, the term axis mundi – also called the cosmic axis, world axis, world pillar, center of the world, or world tree – has been greatly extended to refer to any mythological concept representing "the connection between Heaven and Earth" or the "higher and lower realms". Romanian religious historian Mircea Eliade introduced the concept in the 1950s. Axis mundi closely relates to the mythological concept of the omphalos (navel) of the world or cosmos. It is essentially an imaginary vertical axis or linkage as a central pole, running from the sky through the ground, uniting heaven, earth and underworld. The image is both feminine (an umbilical cord providing nourishment) and masculine (a phallus providing insemination into the uterus). Items adduced as examples of the axis mundi by comparative mythologists include plants (notably a tree but also other types of plants such as a vine or stalk), a mountain, a column of smoke or fire, or a product of human manufacture (such as a staff, a tower, a ladder, a staircase, a maypole, a cross, a steeple, a rope, a totem pole, a pillar, a spire). Its proximity to heaven may carry implications that are chiefly religious (pagoda, temple mount, minaret, church) or secular (obelisk, lighthouse, rocket, skyscraper). The image appears in religious and secular contexts. In Mircea Eliade's opinion: "Every Microcosm, every inhabited region, has a Centre; that is to say, a place that is sacred above all."

The existence of multiple centres is not considered to be a contradiction at all.

In the axis mundi theory, every ancient civilization believed that there is a specific spot where Heaven and Earth have been believed to be connected, or the distance between them has been seen as the smallest. The axis mundi symbol may be found in cultures utilizing shamanic practices or animist belief systems, in major world religions, and in technologically advanced "urban centres".

Mount Kailash as Axis Mundi

As another example, in Hinduism, Mount Meru in India, and Mount Kailash in Tibet, are both regarded as the axis mundi, due to the perceived closeness between heaven and earth.

Depiction of Mount Kailash as axis mundi

Mount Kailash is considered as axis mundi, the centre of the world, with Tibet transecting the axis mundi. Axis mundi, also called world axis or centre of the world, symbolises a point of connection between sky and earth, where the four compass directions of north-east-south-west meet. At this point, travel and correspondence are made between higher and lower realms. Communication from lower realms ascends to higher ones and blessings from higher realms descend to lower ones for dissemination to all. The point functions as the navel of earth, the point of beginning of the world.

Stupas, with the north face of Mount Kailash in the background – both are symbols of axis mundi

Jerusalem as Axis Mundi

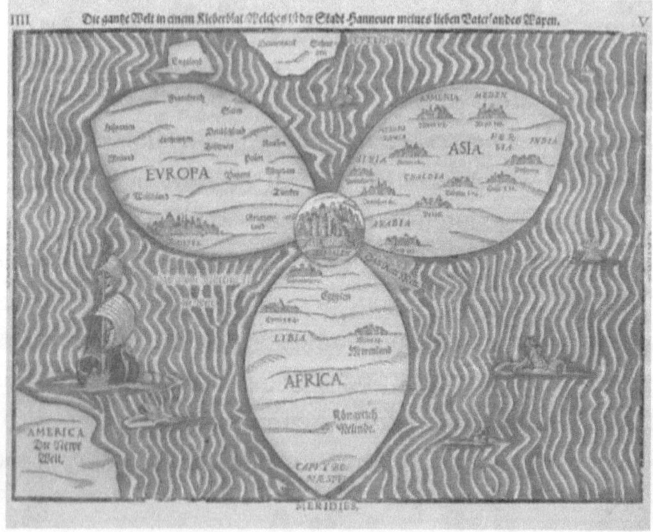

An ancient map of Middle Ages showing Jerusalem as the axis mundi

The ancient Jews considered Jerusalem to be the axis mundi. The ancient Greeks were of the belief that the earth's navel (known as the 'omphalos') existed in several places, most notably at Delphi. In addition, they also believed in a cosmic world tree, as well as Mount Olympus as the dwelling place of their gods.

Nature as Axis Mundi

Nature is the biggest teacher to mankind, and through various means it keeps reminding us of the sacred designs and concepts. There have been sacred mountains considered to be the axis mundi in various religions/civilizations/cultures. Mount Fuji in Japan, Mount Zion in Jerusalem by ancient Jews, Mount Olympus in Greek mythology and the Black Hills of Dakota state in US (by Lakota tribes) are considered as axis mundi. In the case of Chinese civilization, the axis mundi is believed to be the mythological Mount Kunlun, which is regarded in Taoism, as the 'mountain at the middle of the world'.

Bhutanese thangka of Mount Meru and the Buddhist universe, 19th century, Trongsa Dzong

Angkor Wat as Mount Meru and Axis Mundi

The famous Angkor Wat in Cambodia, for instance, was designed by the Khmers to symbolize Mount Meru. This sacred mountain is said to be reflected in the design of the stupas (a mound-like structure normally built to house the relics of the Buddha, or other Buddhist saints) in Buddhism.

Aerial view of Angkor Wat, Siem Reap, Cambodia, 1116-1150 CE

An aerial view of Angkor Wat demonstrates that the temple is made up of an expansive enclosure wall, which separates the sacred temple grounds from the protective moat that surrounds the entire complex. The temple proper is comprised of three galleries (a passageway running along the length of the temple) with a central sanctuary, marked by five stone towers.

The five stone towers are intended to mimic the five mountain ranges of Mount Meru—the mythical home of the gods, for both Hindus and Buddhists. The temple mountain as an architectural design was invented in Southeast Asia. Southeast

Asian architects quite literally envisioned temples dedicated to Hindu gods on earth as a representation of Mount Meru. The galleries and the empty spaces that they created between one another and the moat are envisioned as the mountain ranges and oceans that surround Mount Meru. The mount is not only home to the gods, it is also considered an axis-mundi. In designing Angkor Wat in this way, King Suryavarman II and his architects intended the temple to serve as the supreme abode for Vishnu. Similarly, the symbolism of Angkor Wat serving as axis mundi was intended to demonstrate the Angkor Kingdom's and the king's central place in the universe.

Angkor Wat as Buddhist Mandala

In addition to envisioning Angkor Wat as Mount Meru on earth, the temple's architects also ingeniously designed the temple so that embedded in the temple's construction is a map of the cosmos (Mandala) as well as a historical record of the temple's patron.

According to ancient Sanskrit and Khmer texts, religious monuments and specifically temples must be organized in such a way that they are in harmony with the universe, meaning that the temple should be planned according to the rising sun and moon, in addition to symbolizing the recurrent time sequences of the days, months and years. The central axis of these temples should also be aligned with the planets, thus connecting the structure to the cosmos so that temples become spiritual, political, cosmological, astronomical and geo-physical centres. They are, in other words, intended to represent microcosms of the universe and are organized as Mandalas—diagrams of the universe.

Plants and Trees as Axis Mundi

Plants and trees often serve as images of the axis mundi. The image of the Cosmic Tree provides an axis symbol that unites three planes: sky (branches), earth (trunk), and underworld (roots). In some Pacific Island cultures, the banyan tree – of which the Bodhi tree is of the sacred fig variety – is the abode of ancestor spirits. In Hindu religion, the banyan tree is considered sacred and is called Ashwath Vruksha ("Of all trees I am the banyan tree" – Bhagavad Gita). It represents eternal life because of its seemingly ever-expanding branches.

The Mahabodhi Temple at Bodhgaya, Bihar, India

As per Buddhist texts, the famous Mahabodhi Temple represents Mount Meru. The Bodhi tree is the one under which Gautama Siddhartha Buddha, sat on the night he attained enlightenment.

Humans as Axis Mundi

Situated between the upper and the lower realms, human beings are considered to be a form of axis mundi themselves. The whole chakra system is based on the concept of cosmic pole, where the practitioner with the help of meditation can reach a state of nothingness. In practices of Yoga and Tai Chi Chuan, it is believed that the human body is a temple and the gap between the two extremes can be bridged enabling the human beings to transcend their earthly existence through meditation and prayer. The legendary Renaissance painter Leonardo da Vinci's Vitruvian man represented a symbolic and mathematical exploration of the human form as world axis.

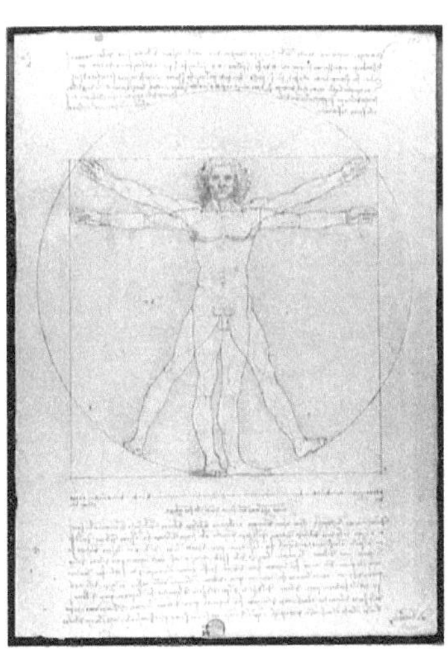

Vitruvian man by Leonardo da Vinci (1490 CE)

CHAPTER 6

Religious Context

Hinduism

Lake Manasarovar and Mount Kailash are most sacred to Hinduism. Kailash is believed to be the abode of Shiva, Parvati, Ganesha and Kartikeya. This is where the holy river the Ganges is believed to be tamed by Shiva and sent to nourish the fertile valleys below the Himalayas. Kailash is sometimes conflated with Meru. For the Khas Hindu shamans of the nearby region of Humla (northwest Nepal), a ritual bath in Lake Manasarovar is an important step in gaining their shamanic powers.

An illustration depicting Shiva, Parvati, Ganesha and Kartikeya at Kailash

Buddhism

Buddhists associate the lake as the mother principle, with Kailash as the father principle. The Yamantaka shrine here is one of the eight guardian deities, who is shown in the act of a sexual embrace to unite compassion and wisdom. A traditional 52 kms (32.5 miles) circumambulation around the mountain, called kora, is believed to be a holy walk. According to legend, Queen Maya bathed at Manasarovar before she gave birth to Buddha.

The Tibetan Buddhists consider Mount Kailash a representation of Buddhist cosmology on earth. Vajrayana Buddhists believe that Mount Kailash is the home of the Buddha Cakrasaṃvara (also known as Demchok), who represents supreme bliss. Numerous sites in the region are associated with Padmasambhava, whose tantric practices in holy sites around Tibet are credited with finally establishing Buddhism as the main religion of Tibet in the 7/8th century CE.

Thangka depicting Mount Kailash

Jainism

In Jainology texts, it is stated that Rishabhadeva (also called Adinath), the first Tirthankara of the 24 in the Jain pantheon, went on a pilgrimage to Kailash mountain area and attained his Moksha or Nirvana at Mount Ashtapada. The text also states that when Vardhamana Mahavira, the 24th and the last Tirthankara was born, God Indra with his retinue came down from heaven, anointed the infant, put the mother Trishala to sleep, took the child to Kailash and Manasarovar to perform Abhisheka (consecration), brought him back to the mother and went back to heaven. Consequently, in Jainism, Kailash – Manasarovar occupy special significance attracting Jain devotees also for the pilgrimage.

Rishabhadeva attained Nirvana on Mount Kailash

Bon religion

The Bon religion is also associated with Mount Kailash as they believe that Tonpa Shenrab, the founder of their religion, landed at Kailash when he descended from heaven and he also bathed in Manasarovar Lake.

CHAPTER 7

Historical Context of Kailash-Manasarovar

There is no mention of the lake or its location in Vedic literature or ancient Sanskrit and Prakrit texts. Though modern texts of the colonial era refer to Manasarovar as among the most sacred sites of Indian religions, particularly Hinduism, this status is not found in Indian texts authored prior to the 10th century CE. The early Buddhist, Hindu and Jain texts mention a mythical Mount Meru and Lake Manasa. The mythical Manasa lake is described as one created through the mind of Brahma, as the preferred abode for his mount/Vahana – Hamsa (swan).

While there is no explicit mention of this lake or the nearby mountain in ancient Sanskrit texts, there is indirect mention of this region of Tibet in hymn 2.15 of the Rigveda. There it says that the Indus River keeps flowing north because of Indra's power, a geographical reality only in Tibet. This is in the context of Himavant (Peak of snow of Himalayas). According to Frits Staal, a Sanskrit and Vedic studies scholar, this makes it likely that some among the ancient Vedic people traced the Indus river route and had seen the valley near Mount Kailash. However, there is no mention of this lake or it being a 'Tirtha' (pilgrimage site).

Traditionally, major historic pilgrimage sites that were frequented by Buddhists, Hindus and Jains attracted discussion in their respective texts, leading to the construction of infrastructures by wealthy patrons or kings. In Hindu texts, these infrastructures are connecting roads, temples, Dharmasalas, Ashramas and pilgrimage facilities on the route. At least until the 1930s, there was no evidence of such structures in the Kailash-Manasarovar region.

The earliest verifiable reports that confirm that this lake site attracted pilgrims are those of the Buddhists. According to the 20th century Italian scholar of Himalayan history Luciano Petech, Tibetan records confirm that Buddhists considered the region, now identified as Kailash and Manasarovar, to be their sacred geography by late 12th-century, with many reports of Buddhist monks meditating in the caves of Mount Kailash and circumambulating the mountain.

According to the renowned research scholar on Indo-Tibetan history Alex McKay, the possible synthesis of esoteric Buddhism and the prevalence of Shaivism in Nepal, Tibet and eastern region of India may have expanded and brought Kailash and lake Manasarovar into the shared sacred geography for both Buddhists and Hindus. The 13th-century text Mahanirvana Tantra dedicates its first chapter to Kailash and Manasarovar lake as a pilgrimage site. This may have been coupled with the re-discovery of its importance of the major rivers in the subcontinent

Between 1901 and 1905, southern Tibet became strategically important to the British Empire. The colonial era officials decided to encourage and assist religious pilgrimage to this lake and Kailash with comments such as "a devotee will be the pioneer of trade". By 1907, about 150 pilgrims a year visited this site, a number significantly higher than those in the 19th century. The number of Indian pilgrims grew to 730 by 1930. Pilgrimage road and facilities to this lake and Kailash were constructed by Indians, in cooperation with Tibetan monks and officials, along the route after 1930.

In May 2020, India inaugurated a new 80 km long motorable road from Dharchula (District Pithoragarh, Uttarakhand) to Lipu Lekh Pass along the India-China border under the geostrategic India-China Border Roads Project to the Kailash-Manasarovar region in Tibet.

CHAPTER 8

Pilgrimage or Yatra: Kailash - Manasarovar: When and How?

Lake Manasarovar and Mount Kailash are visible from the Lapcha La pass, located above the Limi valley in the district of Humla, Nepal. A religious journey performed by a devotee or pilgrim is known as pilgrimage or Yatra. The glistening snow-covered peak of Mount Kailash is among the most breath-taking sights in the world. Despite being one of the most demanding, challenging, adventurous and enduring ventures, the trekkers, hikers and pilgrims from all parts of the world, visit Mount Kailash every year. Kailash – Manasarovar region is also known for its cultural values. The journey through the Kailash – Manasarovar Yatra is divine in itself and on the way, one may experience many different locations/sites, holding some unique and sacred significance in the hearts of the pilgrims. One will also come across lush green valleys, infinitely stretched barren lands, a range of snow-capped mountains and beautiful lakes. The landscape scene is quite risky and the journey turns out to be steep and unpleasant every now and then. Hence, the pilgrims need to be at the best of their health to complete the journey. It is indeed an experience of a lifetime for any nature-lover.

Due to bone-freezing weather, the region remains cold throughout the year. The period of visit is from May till the end of September. However, the ideal time to visit is from April to mid-June and September to mid-October, because the weather is pleasant with no rains, which is the biggest impediment during the trek.

Circumambulation means circling around any particular place or spot. The Sanskrit word for circumambulation of a holy site is 'Parikrama' or 'Pradakshina', and the Tibetan word for the same act is 'Kora'. Both words are widely used to describe, while performing circumambulation of Lake Manasarovar and Mount Kailash. This is the most important part of the pilgrimage. It is believed that any individual who completes the circumambulation will erase the entirety of his/her wrongdoings that he or she might have committed in life.

CHAPTER 9

Pilgrimage: Lake Manasarovar

Lake Manasarovar (also called Mapam Yumtso in Tibetan) is a high altitude freshwater lake with crystal-clear and pristine water. It is also said to be changing colours, from crystal blue near the shores to emerald green in the centre. A full moon night is supposed to be the best and ideal opportunity to see the lake at its best, as it shines like a jewel. The glaciers of Gurla Mandhata mountain with the highest peak at 7694 m (25,243 ft) in the Manasarovar Kailash region feed the lake. The lake, along with Mount Kailash to its north, are sacred sites for the four religions: Hinduism, Jainism, Buddhism and Bon. The Sanskrit word "Manasarovar" is a combination of two Sanskrit words; "Manas" meaning "mind" (in its widest sense as applied to all the mental powers – intellect, intelligence, understanding, perception, sense and conscience), while "Sarovar" means "a lake or a large water body or pond deep enough for a lotus". As per Hinduism, the lake was formed inside the mind of Lord Brahma; hence the name Manasarovar was given to it.

Lake Manasarovar with Gurla Mandhata mountain in the background

Lake Manasarovar has a diameter of 28 kms (17. 5 miles), circumference of 88 kms (54.7 miles), surface area of 320 sq.kms (123.6 sq miles) and a maximum depth of 90 m (300 ft). It is relatively round in shape and is at an altitude of 4530 m (15100 ft) above mean sea level. Manasarovar is connected to nearby Lake Rakshastal by the natural Ganga Chhu channel. Manasarovar overflows into Lake Rakshastal which is a salt-water endorheic lake (drainage basin with no outlet). When the level of Lake Rakshastal matches that of Lake Manasarovar, these very-narrowly-combined lakes overflow into the Sutlej basin. Lake Manasarovar is near the source of the Sutlej, which is the easternmost large tributary of the Indus. Nearby are the sources of the Rivers Brahmaputra, Indus and Karnali, an important tributary of the Ganges.

The trail to Lake Manasarovar

Small temples and stupa near the lake

Prayer flags on the shore

Monuments and Mount Kailash near the lake

There are billions of midges and caddisflies that encircle the lake shore and irritate the pilgrims. The pilgrims take a dip in waist/chest level water at about 5 to 10 m from the lake shore. An interesting belief about the sacred lake is that when you take a holy dip in the pristine waters of Manasarovar, you feel something otherworldly. It is said that the dip can cleanse away all your pains and sorrows and all your negative energies within seconds. Drinking its water or bathing in the lake will again, get your soul as well as your mind, clear of any negative thoughts and will set you on track to attain Nirvana. Many pilgrims claim to have seen several events in their lives or moments from their past after they took a small dip in the freezing waters. This interesting phenomenon has been experienced by many people with reverence and wonder.

Believers and pilgrims who come for the Yatra, believe that completing a full Kora or circumambulation of Lake Manasarovar is an act of wish – fulfilment and it cleanses their souls from all sins of previous hundred years. The circumambulation is done by the pilgrims in vehicles around the lake as roads are motorable. But the orthodox hardy Tibetans believe in doing Kora of the lake on foot.

There are a variety of bird species which thrive on the abundant variety of fishes in the lake, which feed on algae and other weeds in the lake. The bird species are black-headed sea gulls, black-necked cranes and geese. The mythical swans (Hamsa) are also said to be present. During winter months, these birds migrate to the warmer climates of Indian subcontinent as the Siberian cranes also do.

The lake has a few monasteries on its shores, the most notable of which is the ancient Chiu Gompa Monastery. It is built on a steep red-coloured hill, looking as if it has been carved right out of the rock. From this monastery, one can enjoy an amazing view of Lake Manasarovar and Gurla Mandhata peak.

Chiu Gompa Monastery

View of Manasarovar and Gurla Mandhata from Chiu

After the circumambulation of Lake Manasarovar, all pilgrims are advised to rest overnight at the camp near Chiu Gompa Monastery on the lakeshore. This helps them to get acclimatized with the high altitude, before starting the arduous trek of Mount Kailash. Next morning the pilgrims are driven to the base camp of Darchen for the Kailash trek. Darchen is a driving distance of 33 kms from Chiu Gompa camp.

CHAPTER 10

Pilgrimage: Mount Kailash: Parikrama or Kora

The mountain is located in a particularly remote and inhospitable area of the Tibetan Himalayas. Circumambulation of the mountain has to be done on foot, pony or domestic Yak. A few modern amenities, such as benches, resting places, and refreshment kiosks exist to ease the exhaustion of the weary pilgrims. For varied reasons of the different faiths that revere the mountain, setting foot on Mount Kailash's slopes and attempting to climb it is forbidden.

According to Buddhism, one circumambulation around the mountain can erase all the sins committed throughout one's current lifetime. Completing ten circles around the mountain leads to prevention of eternal damnation of hell tribulation in one's reincarnations during 500 years. 108 circles remove the sins of all lifetimes and brings Moksha, salvation from reincarnation. Alternatively, pilgrims who complete one circle of the Kailash and bathe in the frigid waters of Lake Manasarovar, will also attain salvation.

Most Hindu and Buddhist pilgrims take three days to complete the pilgrimage around Mount Kailash, whereas the ancient hardy Bonpos and some Tibetan and Nepali pilgrims from high altitude regions, complete it in two days and some even in one day. Some Bon pilgrims venture a very demanding regimen, performing body-length prostrations over the entire length of the circumambulation. The pilgrim bends down, kneels, prostrates full-length, makes a mark with his/her fingers, rises to the knees, prays, and then crawls forward on hands and knees to the mark made by the fingers before repeating the process. With this method, the pilgrimage takes at least three weeks to complete one Kora. Tibetan and Himalayan Buddhist pilgrims often sing 'Nyelu' songs while crossing the Dolma La pass. These Tibetan songs proclaim the timeless fraternity of all pilgrims who cross paths on a Kailash pilgrimage.

Bon pilgrims performing full body prostrations around Kailash

Due to 40% deficiency in the oxygen level at these high altitudes, as compared to that at mean sea levels, most pilgrims/tourists face severe breathing problems, whereas the Tibetans who are well-acclimatized, do not face any breathing difficulties.

Many pilgrims and tourists get high altitude sickness during the trek. The symptoms are nausea, headache, vomiting and breathlessness. It is therefore essential to consume plenty of water, ORS (Oral Rehydration Salts), glucose, chocolates, dry fruits and energy drinks. Some pilgrims consume a popular energy drink called Red Bull. It is said that a 250 ml drink of Red Bull gives 1000 calories to provide extra energy for the trek. It is said that this drink contains steroid stimulant and makes some people groggy.

Hindus, Tibetan Buddhists, Jains and the folks of Bon religion firmly believe in the divinity of Mount Kailash and have various convictions about the Parikrama. Many pilgrims believe that doing the Parikrama/Kora of Mount Kailash on foot is a spiritually beneficial practice that can bring various positive effects, such as the collection of meritorious Karma, the cleansing of sins from one's consciousness and good fortune. As per the scriptures, one's sins could be erased if one makes a circular trek around the sacred mountain. The circumambulation is made in a clockwise direction by Hindus, Buddhists, and Jains, while Bonpos circumambulate the mountain in a counter-clockwise direction. The total length of a full Kora around the Holy Mountain is 52 kms. There are two types of Parikrama/Kora. The outer Kora trek and the inner Kora trek.

Outer Kora

There is a base camp at Darchen where the pilgrims stay before they start the pilgrimage of Mount Kailash. After arriving at Darchen camp from Chiu Gompa, the pilgrim is advised to take rest for one day/night at Darchen for acclimatization.

5 kms from here is Tarboche on the southern face of Mount Kailash. The actual trek of Kailash Kora starts from Yam Dwar at Tarboche. Unlike the Tibetans, our bodies are not programmed to be trekking in such high altitudes and in such light breathing conditions. Hence the Kailash Kora of 52 kms is divided into 3 days, with rest during night halts at two camps.

Day 1

The first day's trek is about 18 kms with the route not being very steep. The trek is through Sarshung Village, Lha Chu Valley and Chuku/Choku Monastery. Views of Kailash and other mountains around, flowing streams and placid lakes are breath-taking. Some of the lakes are frozen. The trek route is strewn with pebbles and stones with little ups and downs. One just needs to stick together with the group at all points. A night halt at a meadow near a monastery at Dira Puk, at altitude of 5210 m (16,010ft), enables the trekkers to rest. The best view of north face of Kailash is possible from Dira Puk. This view from Dira Puk is truly magnificent.

Many stones on the Kailash path

Day 2

The second day's trek of 22 kms is across a rocky field, which is also a sky burial site for pilgrims who have died during Kora. (The Tibetans follow the custom of leaving the dead bodies on high mountain tops to disintegrate and merge with the earth, known as sky burial). The second day's trek is extremely arduous and the most daunting, tiring and challenging out of the three days. The trek is quite dangerous, with steep and drastic ascents and descents, where one needs to be very careful. It follows a rough and rugged terrain. It takes one through Shivasthal to the Dolma La Pass, which, at 5650 m (18,540 ft), is the highest point of the trek. It is advised not to stay at the Dolma La pass for much long since the thin air and strong cold winds could be harmful. The Tibetans believe that a person crossing Dolma La is rid of all sins and gets a rebirth. To signify this, many chop off and discard their hairs, cast away the old clothes they wear and change to new set of clothes. A 100 m after Dolma La Pass is the holy Gauri Kund (also called Parvati Sarovar) at 5610 m (18,400 ft), where Parvati is said to have bathed. Lam Chu valley and a descent follow Gauri Kund. Further, it is level trekking for the last 9 kms to reach the second rest point at Zutul Puk at altitude of 4790 m (15,780 ft), near another monastery.

Day 3

The distance from Zutul Puk to Darchen is 12 kms. On the third day, after visiting the 11th century cave of the Buddhist monk Milarepa nearby, going down the Dzing chu valley and turning west, one reaches Chongdo, which is 8 kms from Zutul Puk. From here, since the road is motorable, the waiting vehicles pick up the pilgrims and drop them at Darchen camp, which is just 4 kms away.

Kailash Kora route – Outer (Blue) and Inner (Red)

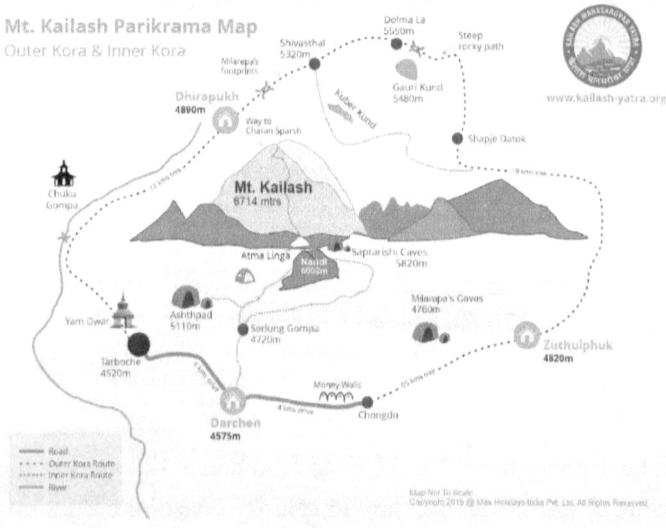

Source: MaxHoldiays.com

Inner Kora

The inner Kora is relatively smaller and is 34 kms, compared to the 52 kms of outer Kora. But the inner Kora of Kailash is infinitely more arduous than the outer Kora. There are three legs in the inner Kora.

The first leg of 6 kms starts from Dira Puk Monastery just to cover Charan Sparsh. The second leg of 18 kms from Shivasthal covers Kuber valley and Kuber Kund and reaches Zutul Puk. The third leg starts from the northern side of Darchen, goes via Selung Monastery to do a loop or Kora around Nandi Parvat, covers Ashtapada cave, Atma Linga and Saptarishi caves and reaches Gyangzha or Gyandrak Monastery. During this trek, there is a platform from where one can view the famous naturally formed 'ice Swastika'. It is formed by the ice cracks on the southern side of Mount Kailash. Hundreds of Tibetan prayer flags can be seen flapping uncontrollably in the chill winds. Also, 13 chortens can be seen on the route to Gyangzha Monastery, which are the final resting places of 13 former Gyangzha administrators. Gyangzha Monastery at 5060 m, is said to be established as early as 13th century. It is said to be the first monastery in Kailash region. This leg covers a trek of 10 kms with a night halt on the route.

The inner Kora treks can be completed in one or two days, but many tourists don't prefer the inner trek, as there are a lot of cliffs, high altitude passes and glaciers to hike over. Another reason why very few people take the inner trek is because, Buddhists believe that to qualify to do the inner Kora, one has to do the outer Kora 13 times. Also, since foreigners are not permitted to undertake the inner Kora and is restricted to only a few pilgrims with special permits from the administration, most pilgrims and adventure tourists/trekkers do only the outer Kora.

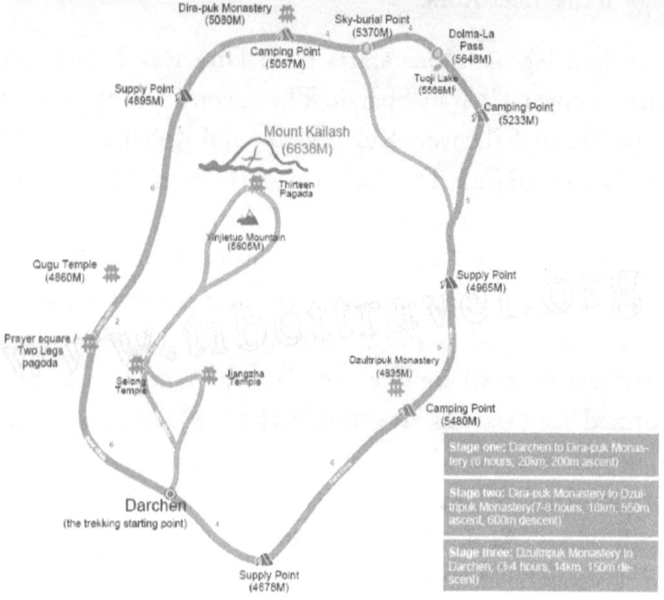

Kailash Kora Route – Outer (Orange) and Inner (Blue)
https://www.tibettravel.org/blog/western-tibet-travel/

Monasteries around Mount Kaiiash

There are totally five monasteries surrounding Mount Kailash – three in the outer circuit and two in the inner circuit. These monasteries have old relics, statues, thangkas, etc. They also offer simple accommodation.

1. Chuku/Choku/Nyari Monastery – Chuku Monastery is one of the five monasteries surrounding Mount

Kailash. Located at an altitude of 4875 m and 2 kms from Tarboche, it stands on the side of a cliff on the bank of River Lha Chu. The main attraction in this monastery is the statue of Buddha Opame which is made of stone. There is also a Thangka image of Chuku Rinpochu. Other things worthy of mention in this monastery are silver embossed tea pots and conch shells. There is no entry fee and the monastery is open on all days.

2. Dira Puk Monastery – Dira Puk Monastery is located at an altitude of 5210 m and is one of the monasteries that provide food and a resting place for the pilgrims. The word 'Dira Puk' means 'cave of a female horn' referencing the paintings of horns on the walls. There are a few murals, paintings, and Buddha statues in the monastery.

3. Zutul Puk Monastery – Zutul Puk Monastery is located at an altitude of 4790 m. It is 11kms from Darchen. With a lush valley around, the scenery and view outside this monastery are amazing. A feeling of calm and serenity prevails which soothe the tired pilgrims, who reach here after the arduous trek on the second day. The accommodation in Zutul Puk is considered to be the best during the Kora.

4. Selung Monastery – Standing at an elevation of 5020 m, Selung monastery is one of the highest monasteries of Mount Kailash. It is located closer to the inner Kora route. From this monastery, after a few hundred metres, one can see the natural Swastika formed by ice cracks on the south face of Mount Kailash. This monastery, which is mostly in ruins, also serves as a meditating and resting place for pilgrims.

5. Gyangzha or Gyandrak Monastery – Gyangzha Monastery is the oldest and most important monastery in the Mount Kailash region. It stands at an altitude of 5075 m and was established in the 13th century. The monastery has some interesting relics and murals. The architecture of the monastery is different from that of others.

Holy spots on the Kora

It has been rightly said, "The Journey is the most memorable part of the trip." And on this great mix of a spiritual and an adventurous journey, one comes across many different divine spots or spiritual hubs which are associated with immense sanctity. The important holy spots on the Kailash Yatra are explained below:

Rakshas Tal

Rakshas Tal, meaning "Lake of devil", carries many mysterious tales and folklores regarding the Demon King – Ravana. At 4575 m (15,010 ft), It is situated near the Lake Manasarovar and is the sole saltwater lake in Tibet, believed to comprise of poisonous gases. Earlier, it used to be a part of Lake Manasarovar, but due to tectonic movements and geographical shifts, the two lakes got separated. A thin isthmus of mountains separates them now, as if differentiating the good and the bad. The Rakshas Tal is said to be the dwelling place of Ravana and thus, is of great historical and spiritual relevance.

Darchen

Darchen is the starting and ending point for the Kora. It does not have much religious significance attached to it, but serves as an accommodation camp. There are camps or local guesthouses for accommodation and to relax the mind and soul after the tiring climb and descent around the mountain. It is at an elevation of 4670 m (15,320 ft). It is situated right in front of the mountain and is basically a small village outpost that swells with pilgrims at certain times of the year, during the pilgrimage season. Darchen is surrounded by several varieties of tea shops, to enable people to stay warm in this dreadfully cold climate. Due to its location, people travelling on a Kailash Manasarovar Yatra need to rest here, both on arrival and before departure. Those who do not want to go further on the strenuous trek around Kailash, can stay here for a few days before heading back home with the group.

Tarboche

Tarboche at an elevation of 4575 m (15,500 ft), is the entry point to Mount Kailash. It is at a driving distance of 5 kms from Darchen. Tibetan People believe that Kailash is the home of 'Demchok', who is considered to be their deity. Therefore, every year, before commencement of the pilgrimage season, they ceremoniously erect a new 24 m (80 ft) high flag-pole, full of Tibetan prayer-flags. The colourful Tibetan flags have their deep meaning. They arrange the flags in a specific colour sequence, which is "blue, white, red, green, yellow", from left to right. Blue coloured flag is a representation of the sky, the white colour is of air, the red colour is of fire, the green colour is of water and the yellow colour is of earth, thus representing Panchabhutas, the five great elements, of which every human is made up of. Therefore, all these flags together represent the balance establishing life on earth. It is an entrance that a devil or evil power may never pass through. It is thus believed that the pilgrims are protected from any harm by devil or evil powers.

Tibetan prayer flags at Tarboche pole with Mount Kailash in background
Source: Gettyimages

Yam Dwar

At Tarboche, the entrance gate called "Yam Dwar" stands prominently. In Hinduism, Lord Yama, popularly referred to as Yamraj, is the god of death. 'The Gateway to the God of Death' and 'The Gate of Salvation' are few of the names given to the mysterious Yam Dwar. Therefore, it has a prominent position and significance. All pilgrims proceeding on the pilgrimage trek around the holy Mount Kailash, have to pass through this gate, signifying that they are rid of their sins and can achieve Nirvana. While passing through this gate, people tend to pray to 'Yama', for successfully completing their pilgrimage and also for passing through the gate on their death in their spiritual form. It is believed that on completion of circumambulation of Mount Kailash, an individual is assured of a place in heaven, as all his sins/evil deeds are erased.

Yam Dwar

As per the Hindu belief, Lord Yama himself guards the abode of Lord Shiva. His retinues bring the mortal souls of all people to Yamlok. Yama has the duty to judge one's deeds after one's death, based on the merits earned and sins committed. Chitragupta is the accountant of Yamlok. He keeps accounts of all good and bad deeds of each and every individual. In Hindu Mythology, there are many stories about the Yam Dwar that proves how much auspicious and powerful this Dwar is.

As per another Hindu belief, if you just complete the circumambulation of Yam Dwar itself, it is as good as circumambulation of Mount Kailash. Chitragupta then removes all your sins/evil deeds from the book of judgment.

Nandi Parvat

Nandi is Lord Shiva's sacred mount or vehicle, represented by the holy Nandi Parvat. It is considered to be an important peak in the Kailash Yatra holding utmost divinity and is reachable in the inner Kora. Nandi is said to be born as human, but is depicted as a half-man half-bull or a bull sitting with its limbs folded. He was to die at the age of 8, and so he started worshipping Lord Shiva with great devotion and passion. This made Lord Shiva happy and he gave a necklace with an attached bell to Nandi, transforming him into half-human half-bull and making him immortal. It is said that Nandi is the hub of powers, provider of boons, a true symbol of honour, justice, faith, wisdom and boldness and also the protector of Dharma.

Ashtapada

Ashtapada is considered to be one of the most splendid pilgrimage spots for the tourists and pilgrims in the inner Kora circuit. It is known as the place where the first Tirthankara of Jains, Rishabhadeva, achieved Nirvana and thus, the spot is very significant to the Jain religion. Ashtapada literally means eight steps indicating the eight mountain peaks on this religious or divine spot. Amongst all the destinations or places falling in between the Kailash – Manasarovar Yatra, Ashtapada is said to be the most beautiful due to the natural scenic views and the positive holy vibrations present at this place.

Gauri Kund/Parvati Sarovar

Also called Parvati Sarovar, Gauri Kund comes during the trek from Dira Puk camp towards Zutul Puk camp, in the outer Kora circuit. A plethora of tales and folklores about Lord Shiva and Goddess Parvati are associated with Gauri Kund. It is one of the most winsome lakes across the globe. Referred to as "The Lake of Compassion", it is tucked at an elevation of around 5608 m (18,400 ft) above sea level. According to the ancient tale in the holy Shiva Purana, it is said that Gauri Kund is the place where Goddess Parvati was able to get back her son – Lord Ganesha. Gauri Kund is said to be an essential spot to be seen by all the pilgrims of the Kailash Yatra. The splashing of the water of the Kund is believed to purify one's senses and soul.

CHAPTER 11

Mountaineering

In 1926, Hugh Ruttledge studied the north face, which he estimated was 6,000 feet (1,800 m) high and "utterly unclimbable" and thought about an ascent of the northeast ridge, but he ran out of time. Ruttledge had been exploring the area with Colonel R. C. Wilson, who was on the other side of the mountain with his Sherpa named Tseten. Wilson said that Tseten told him: 'Sahib, we can climb that!'... as he too saw that the southeast ridge represented a feasible route to the summit." Wilson went on to explain that although he was serious about climbing Kailash, he ran into unexpected difficulties: "Just when I discovered an easy walk to the summit of the mountain, heavy snow began to fall, making the ascent impossible."

Herbert Tichy was in the area in 1936, attempting to climb Gurla Mandhata. When he asked one of the Garpons of Ngari whether Kailash was climbable, the Garpon replied: "Only a man entirely free of sin could climb Kailash. And he wouldn't have to actually scale the sheer walls of ice to do it – he'd just turn himself into a bird and fly to the summit."

Reinhold Messner was given the opportunity by the Chinese government to climb in the mid-1980s. But he declined, saying "If we conquer this mountain, then we conquer something in people's souls."

In 2001, reports emerged that the Chinese government had given permission for a Spanish team to climb the peak, which caused an international backlash. Chinese authorities disputed the reports, and stated that any climbing activities on Mount Kailash were strictly prohibited.

CHAPTER 12

Routes to Kailash-Manasarovar

Season for Pilgrimage

Kailash – Manasarovar pilgrimage journey, called Yatra, is considered the pinnacle of religious destinations for Hindu pilgrims. This Yatra is different because there are no well – built temples, shrines or comfort facilities in the traversing path that leads to the mountain. Every year, Kailash pilgrimage is possible only between April and mid-October. April-June and September-October are recommended periods for the pilgrimage; in July and August, monsoonal rains can make the circumambulation somewhat challenging. Between late October and early April, the winter conditions can be extremely severe in this high, windswept corner of Tibet, and generally make the pilgrimage impossible. For all foreigners, including pilgrims from India and Nepal, passports and specific Chinese visas valid for the Kailash pilgrimage are necessary.

Modern/Present Day Pilgrimage with Tibet under Chinese Control

The pilgrimage to Manasarovar and Kailash has been going on since very ancient times. However, from 1949, when China became a communist state, till 1980, Tibet, including Kailash-Manasarovar, was closed to tourists and pilgrims from outside China. From 1980 onwards, tourists and pilgrims are allowed to visit Kailash-Manasarovar areas with special permits. Since the 1980s, the numbers of pilgrims going on a Kailash pilgrimage annually has grown considerably. In 2007, over 70,000 people visited the area around Mount Kailash and Lake Manasarovar. Most of them were pilgrims, and these included about 18,000 foreign visitors (foreign here implying non-Tibetan/non-Chinese). In the years just before the COVID-19 pandemic, several thousand pilgrims from India were going to this pilgrimage every year, mostly through Nepal. While many more aspire to undertake this pilgrimage, it remains out of reach for most due to high expenses; the risks and difficulties posed by the remoteness of Mount Kailash and the high-altitude of the pilgrimage route, and the unpredictable closures of this pilgrimage due to adverse developments in the regional geopolitics.

Climate change

Climate change due to global warming is happening three times faster on the Tibetan Plateau than anywhere else in the world. Mount Kailash is located in a mountain range upon the Tibetan Plateau, near the plateau's western edges. According to local observers, the land around Mount Kailash has been growing warmer in recent years; the pilgrimage season isn't as cold as it used to be. According to available data from the region, glaciers are retreating, lakes are shrinking, the amount of barren land is increasing, and the eventual thawing of the permafrost in this region may lead to uncertain effects on water resources and carbon cycles. The intergovernmental organisation ICIMOD (International Centre for Integrated Mountain Development) is involved in ongoing efforts to generate knowledge on the ecological, social, and economic effects of climate change, and sustainable ways to cope with them, in the Chinese region around Mount Kailash and the bordering areas of Uttarakhand (India) and western Nepal, in a transboundary project called the Kailash Sacred Landscape Conservation and Development Initiative.

Road conditions in Tibet

The roads in Tibet for the pilgrims are in a bad condition. The roads, if they can be called so, are really dusty paths through stone-strewn, rough, barren areas, raising large clouds of dust when vehicles ply. There are far too many diversions every now and then due to construction of culverts and bridges on the route. Massive road construction projects, with heavy earth-moving machinery such as Komatsu, have been undertaken by the Chinese Government. The only passenger vehicle which plies in this rough terrain is Toyota landcruiser, which has a powerful engine of 4.5 litre capacity and 4-wheel drive. This rugged cross-country vehicle is capable of manoeuvring and negotiating this road-less terrain. However, during the road journey through this inhospitable terrain, splendid scenic views can be enjoyed by travellers.

As Kailash Manasarovar is situated at elevations above 4600 m (15,000 ft), the pilgrims should ensure before starting the journey, that they are quite healthy and fit. Also, they have to carry with them sufficient water, food, woollens and clinical supplies.

Other than the Lipu Lekh route through India and the Humla route through Nepal, all the major routes to Kailash involve 3-4 days of long drives through the high-altitude Tibetan plateau and some mountain ranges on it, to reach to Darchen.

From Nepal the routes are through Kodari-Zhangmau or Raswagarh-Gyirang border checkposts. From Tibet, the route is from Lhasa, Zhangmau, Gyirong, and Nathu La.

In descending order of size and development, the cities/towns in Tibet are Lhasa, X'gatse/Shigatse, Nyalam, Saga, Darchen and Prayang.

Road Links to Kailash-Manasarovar

Kailash-Manasarovar is reachable only by roads which are connected to various entry points to Tibet. The road linkages from Kailash-Manasarovar to these entry points are as below:

a.   The popular road link to Nepal is through Prayang, Saga and Nyalam to Kathmandu through the border between China and Nepal over the Sino-Nepal Friendship Bridge over Bhode Kosi River between the towns of Zhangmau on the Chinese side and Kodari on the Nepal side.

b.   This road also links Lhasa, the capital of Tibet from Saga, through Lhatse and X'gatse/Shigatse.

c.   This same road has another link from Saga to Lazi and Kangma to Nathu La.

d.   There is another road from Darchen through Taklakot to Hilsa, which is the shortest, as it is less than 100 kms. Hilsa is a tri-junction where the borders of India, Nepal and Tibet meet and is reachable in just one day. The Chinese border check post is near the bridge at Hilsa over Karnali River. On crossing to Nepal, the road goes to Nepalgunj via Simikot.

Routes through India Organized by Ministry of External Affairs
www.kailash-yatra.org

Indian pilgrims have the option of going either through the annual Kailash pilgrimages organised by the Government of India's Ministry of External Affairs (MEA), or through private groups organised by various travel companies. For the pilgrimages organised by the Government of India, a person has to be an Indian citizen with a passport valid for at least six months as on September 1 of the current year, besides certain other conditions. The selection of candidates by the government is done through a "fair computer-generated, random, gender-balanced selection process", through which the selected candidates are also assigned either of the two routes to Kailash currently open through India: the Lipu Lekh Pass in Uttarakhand and the Nathu La Pass in Sikkim. In both routes, the entry to China/Tibet is direct from India and not through Nepal.

The pilgrims need to undergo some medical tests before the start of the Yatra by ITBP Hospital and Delhi Heart & Lung Institute (DHLI) to ensure the physical and mental fitness. No private travel companies are allowed to conduct the Kailash-Manasarovar pilgrimage via these two routes.

In each batch of Kailash Manasarovar Yatra organised by the Government of India, an Indian government official accompanies the group as Liaison Officer.

The Lipu Lekh route involves briefing and medical checks in Delhi. The pilgrims then take the road to the Lipu Lekh Pass and beyond to Tibet for the Yatra. Till recently, the Lipu Lekh route required 5-7 days of trekking along the Indian side of the Mahakali valley from Narayan Ashram till the Lipu Lekh Pass. Thereafter, the pilgrims travelled by landcruisers to Taklakot and Darchen. In 2020, the Indian government inaugurated a new motorable road to Lipu Lekh Pass through the Indian side of the Mahakali valley (Kali River marks the border between India and Nepal) to reach the border check-post to enter Tibet. Due to this development, the arduous trek is not needed by the pilgrims now, making it much more convenient for the pilgrims to Mount Kailash via Taklakot.

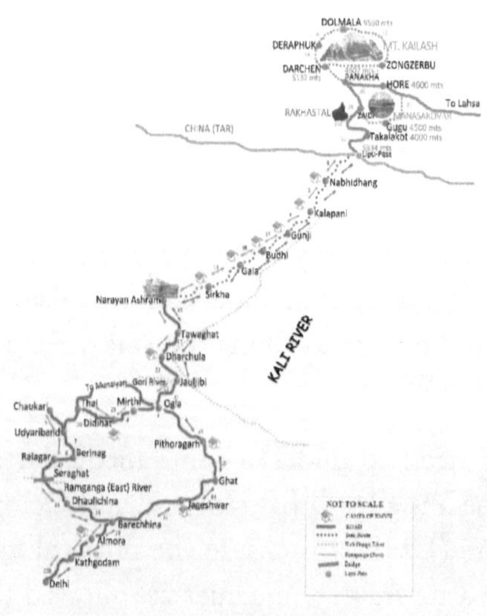

Lipu Lekh Route

The Nathu La route involves briefing and medical checks in Delhi and then a flight from Delhi to Bagdogra. From Bagdogra onwards the Yatra is by road only first to Gangtok, then to Nathu La Pass via Gangtok and thereafter to Sherthang and cross over to China. It takes three days of drive with halts at Kangma village in China, Lazi, Saga / Zhongba, till arrival in Darchen on the fourth day. This route joins the traditional Nepal route at Saga after Lazi.

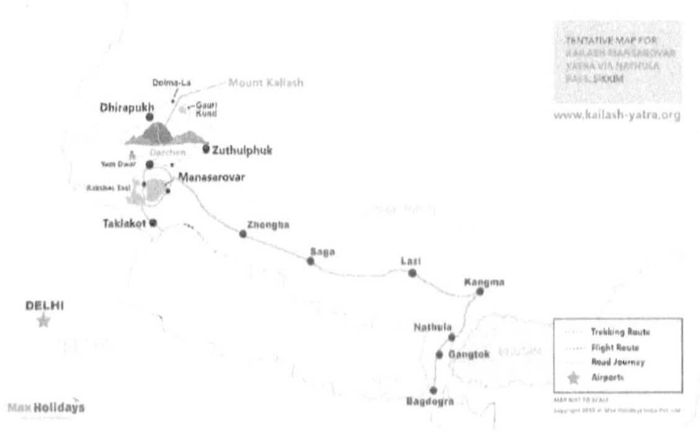

Nathu La route
Source: MaxHolidays.com

Routes through Nepal

The groups organised by travel companies usually go through Nepal. People from all nationalities can go in these groups. Anyone who has the valid documents and can pay, can go with such groups. Generally, there are fewer medical requirements involved in going to Kailash-Manasarovar with private travel companies.

The old route through Nepal is by crossing over Sino-Nepal Friendship bridge at Kodari-Zhangmau over Bhode Kosi River to enter Nyalam county in Tibet and passing through

Saga, Zhongba and reaching Manasarovar/Darchen, taking three days with overnight halts.

A second route through Nepal is the Rasuwagarh-Gyirong route. In this again, Gyirong (Kerung) to Manasarovar/Darchen is a three-day drive.

In recent years, another new route via Nepal is through the Humla district in north-western Nepal. This route involves three flights: Kathmandu-Nepalgunj, Nepalgunj-Simikot, and Simikot-Hilsa (Simikot-Hilsa by helicopter). From Hilsa, the group crosses into Tibet (China). Hilsa to Darchen can be done within a single day. But generally, groups acclimatize at Taklakot for a night, and also tend to stay at Chiu Gumpa by the shores of Lake Manasarovar for a night, before arriving at Darchen.

Routes through Tibet

For private travel companies, both in Nepal and in Tibet (China), another important route to Kailash is the one via Lhasa. In this one, pilgrims first arrive at Lhasa by road, flight or other means, and from there they make a four-day road journey to Lake Manasarovar/Darchen via Shigatse, Lhatse, Saga and Zhongba/Prayang.

Kailash-Manasarovar by Road Itinerary

A typical itinerary of the pilgrimage by road starting from Kathmandu is as below

Day 1

Arrival at Kathmandu and rest

Day 2

Local visits

Day 3

Drive to Kodari-Zhangmau and rest

Day 4

Cross over to Tibet and drive to Nyalam and rest

Day 5

Drive to Saga and rest

Day 6

Drive to Prayang and rest

Day 7

Drive to Manasarovar, Parikrama of lake and rest at Chiu Gompa on the lakeshore

Drive 8

Drive to Darchen and rest

Day 9

Drive to Tarboche and Kora to Dira Puk and rest

Day 10

Kora to Zutul Puk via Dolma La Pass and rest

Day 11

Trek/Drive to Darchen and rest

Day 12

Drive to Prayang and rest

Drive 13

Drive to Nyalam and rest

Day 14

Drive to Zhangmau and rest

Drive 15

Cross over and drive to Kathmandu and rest

Day 16

Departure from Kathmandu

Kailash – Manasarovar By Train

A journey by road is not an option as the nearest rail heads are Lucknow, Kathgodam etc in India. From here, one has to go by road only through Nepal to Tibet.

Kailash – Manasarovar By Air

The pilgrimage by air takes the shortest duration of 9 days and minimum travel distance by the rugged terrain of Tibet. The most convenient airport from where one can start the Yatra is Lucknow in India or Kathmandu in Nepal. The itinerary is as below:

Day 1

Arrive at Lucknow. Drive to Nepalgunj and rest

If arrival is at Kathmandu, fly to Nepalgunj and rest

Day 2

Fly to Simikot and further to Hilsa by helicopter. Cross over to Tibet at Hilsa and drive to Taklakot and rest

Day 3

Rest for acclimatization

Day 4

Drive to Darchen and rest

Day 5

Drive to Tarboche and Kora trek to Dira Puk and rest

Day 6

Kora trek to Zutul Puk crossing Dolma La Pass and rest

Day 7

Drive around Manasarovar and Drive to Hilsa via Taklakot, cross over and rest at Hilsa

Day 8

Fly by helicopter to Simikot and fly to Nepalgunj and rest

Day 9

Drive to Lucknow OR fly to Kathmandu

CHAPTER 13

Panch Kailash

"Panch Kailash", literally meaning "Five Kailashas", is the collective name for the group of five sacred mountain peaks in separate locations in Himalayas, each of which has Kailash in its name. The first most sacred is the Mount Kailash in Tibet. The second most sacred is the "Adi Kailash" in Uttarakhand in India. Om Parvat, a separate mount, is also considered quite sacred and is quite close to Adi Kailash, and is approached through a small diversion from the route to Adi Kailash route. The third, fourth and fifth most sacred are Shikhar Kailash (Shrikhand Mahadev Kailash), Kinnaur Kailash and Manimahesh Kailash, all three in Himachal Pradesh state of India. These are briefly covered in the following paragraphs:

Adi Kailash

Adh Kailash or Adi Kailash (literally Half Kailash), also called Little Kailash, Chhota Kailash, Shiva Kailash or Baba Kailash is a mountain in the Himalayan range near Sinla Pass and Brahma Parvat. It is at an elevation of 5945 m (19,505 ft) in Pithoragarh district of Uttarakhand state in India. It is the second most important peak among the group of Panch Kailash. Its appearance is distinctly similar to Mount Kailash in Tibet.

The base camp of Adi Kailash is 17 km from the Kuthi village in Kuthi Valley at Parvati Tal and Jonglingkong Lake (also called Gaurikund) which has a Shiva temple on its bank. Adi Kailash comes quite close to the route taken by pilgrims to Mount Kailash in Tibet by the ancient traditional route through Kumaon Hills and the Indo-Tibetan Border Police check post between India and Tibet. In May 2020, India inaugurated a new 80 km long road from Dharchula, Pithoragarh district, via Gunji to Lipu Lekh Pass on India-China border, under geostrategic India-China Border Roads project. In July 2020, India also opened a newly constructed road in this area from Gunji to Limpiyadhura Pass on Indo-Tibet border, which has reduced the trek time to Adi Kailash to two hours.

Adi Kailash

Om Parvat at an elevation is 5,590 m (18,340 ft) is nearby and many have a conception that they are one and the same. But they are actually different. The snow deposition pattern on Om Parvat resembles the Hindu sacred symbol AUM/OM (ॐ) and is therefore it is considered sacred by Hindus. Near to Om Parvat is Jonglingkong Lake or Gaurikund. The Hindus consider Jonglingkong lake to be as sacred as Manasarovar.

Om Parvat

Roads are motorable up to Gunji. From Gunji, Adi Kailash is south-west and Om Parvat is north-east. Most trekkers and pilgrims to Adi Kailash also take the diversion from Gunji to Om Parvat for getting an excellent view of the AUM/OM symbol.

The first attempt to climb Adi Kailash was made in Sep-Oct 2002 by an Indo-Aussie-British-Scottish team. It had to be abandoned 200 m (660 ft) short of the summit because of very loose snow and rocky conditions. The first successful ascent of Adi Kailash was in October, 2004 by a team of USA, UK and Scotland mountaineers. They did not ascend the final few steps out of respect for the sacred nature of the summit.

Shikhar Kailash (Shrikhand Mahadev Kailash)

Shikhar Kailash, also called Shrikhand Mahadev Kailash, is a Hindu pilgrimage site in Kullu, Himachal Pradesh, which is considered to be an abode of Lord Shiva and Goddess Parvati.

There is a 23 m (75 ft) tall Shivaling at the top of the Shrikhand Mahadev mountain, at a height of 5715 m (18,570 ft).

The trek to the Shivaling is considered to be one of the toughest treks in India. The starting point for the trek is at Jaon, from where the Shikhar is 32 kms. 3 kms from Jaon is Singhaad, the first base camp where tent accommodation and food are available. From Jaon, there is a 12 km straight uphill stretch to Thaachru, also known as 'Dandi-Dhaar' (roughly translating to Stick-Height), because of the climb being a very steep one with an elevation angle of approximately 70 degrees. One gets to see lush green Deodar trees and streams on the way to Thaachru. After this long, tiring trek, the pilgrim reaches the halting camp at Thaachru.

Next day, the journey begins with a 3 km uphill trek to Kali Ghati, which is supposed to be abode of the Goddess Kali. The Shivaling can be seen from this point, when the weather is clear. From Kali Ghati, there is a 1 km downhill stretch towards Bheem Talai. From Bheem Talai, there is a 3 km stretch to Kunsa Valley, a green valley with Himalayan flowers surrounding it. After another 3 km stretch from here, one reaches the next camp at Bheem Dwaar.

Nain Sarovar

Just 2 km ahead is another camp, Parvati Bagh (Parvati's garden), supposedly a garden planted by Hindu Goddess Parvati. The garden has flowers like Brahma Kamal, which supposedly was used by Lord Shiva to plant an elephant's head on Ganesha (whose head was severed earlier). Ganesha is known as the god of "New Beginnings". 2 kms from there, there is a holy lake known as Nain Sarovar (meaning, Eye's Lake), and revered by numerous people, who have experienced physical healing of old diseases and impairments, after their dip in the lake. Beyond this, is the final stretch of approximately 3 km to the peak, through rocky terrains, where the Shivaling is situated. Nearby, behind Shivaling peak, there is another mountain of Lord Kartikeya.

75 ft Shivaling at the top of the peak

Kinnaur Kailash

The Kinnaur Kailash (locally known as Kinner Kailash) is a mountain in the Kinnaur district of the Indian state of Himachal Pradesh. It is located in proximity to the Indo-Tibetan border. Kinnaur is known as the land of the gods. Its peak is at a height of 6050 m (20,170 ft). It is also among the remotest and the least explored regions of Himachal Pradesh, which is breathtakingly scenic. As per Hindu mythology, Lord Shiva and goddess Parvati reside in Kinnaur Kailash. It is deeply revered by both Hindus and Buddhist Kinnauris residing here.

Kinnaur Kailash Mountain

Religious Significance

For the ardent devotees of Lord Shiva, Kinnaur holds utmost religious significance, since there is a monolithic 24 m (79 ft) rock pointing skywards. It is basically a rock pillar, neatly balanced on a rock slab located at an elevation of around 4800 m (16,000 ft). It is in the shape of the sacred Shivling or Trishul (trident). The speciality about this rock is that it can be seen with variation of colours during the course of the day. When the sun rises, the colour of this rock seems whitish. As sun goes up, its colour varies to reddish during mid – day, pale grey in the evening and dark grey at the sunset. Tourists love to trek to Kinnaur Kailash Mountain to view the mesmerizing beauty of this spot.

Close by, is Parvati Kund, which is located at an elevation of 4470 m (14,900 ft). As per the local folklore, the Kund was created by Goddess Parvati herself and it was the meeting point of Lord Shiva and the goddess and therefore known as 'Aashiqi Park'. As per another mythological belief, every winter, Lord Shiva conducts a meeting of gods and goddesses here.

Colours of Kinnaur Kailash Shivaling

Kinnaur Kailash Parikrama

The Kinnaur Kailash Parikrama (circumambulation) is the most popular trek here. The 14 km long trek is undoubtedly arduous and tough, but is magically rewarding too. Considered as one of the most challenging treks, the trekker/pilgrim is rewarded with beautiful majestic views of the surroundings and pristine nature. The mind-boggling views of snow-clad cold mountains, lush green apple orchards and spectacular landscape are truly unique. The trek will take one through the gorgeous Hangrang Valley and Sangla Valley, where nature can be experienced in its purest form.

The starting point of this trail is Tangling Village (base camp) and ends at Sangla village. This beautiful hamlet is located on the banks of the Sutlej River. From there, the trekker can either take the exciting, but dangerous, Jhoola Pul (the hanging bridge) or the Shongtong Bridge. From Tangling to Maling Khata is 8 kms and Parvati Kund is another 5 kms. Another 1 km trek will take one to the Shivaling rock. The trek takes minimum two to three days to complete, with climb to the Shivaling rock. The best time for the trek is between the months of May and September.

Manimahesh Kailash

The Manimahesh Kailash (also called Chamba Kailash) Peak is at an elevation of 5,653 m (18,547 ft). It is believed that Lord Shiva created Manimahesh after he married Goddess Parvati, who is worshipped as Mata Girija. The peak is believed to be the abode of Lord Shiva. A rock formation in the form of a Shivaling on this mountain is considered as the manifestation of Lord Shiva. There are many other legends, linking Lord Shiva and his show of displeasure through avalanches and blizzards that occur in the region. It towers high over the Manimahesh Lake (also called Dal Lake), which is at an elevation of 4080 m (13,400 ft). The local people consider the snow field at the base of the mountain as Shiva's Chaugan (play field).

The peak is in the Pir Panjal range of Himalayas in the Budhil valley of Bharmour subdivision of Chamba district of Himachal Pradesh. The distance from Bharmour to Manimahesh is 35 kms. Many Hindus, particularly the Gaddi tribe of the region, consider Manimahesh Kailash and Manimahesh Lake to be as sacred as Mount Kailash and Manasarovar of Tibet. It is one of the major pilgrimage sites as well as a popular trekking destination in Himachal Pradesh.

Manimahesh Kailash Peak

Legends

Several mythical legends abound on the sanctity of this peak and the lake at its base.

a. It is said that once a Gaddi tried to climb the peak. He dreamt of Lord Shiva calling him to the peak, asking him to cut the sheep on every step he takes, but told him not to look back. He started to climb the peak step after step and kept cutting the lambs he was carrying with him. But a few steps before reaching the peak, he got confused that he was not carrying many sheep he killed and looked back. He instantly turned into stone. Since then, no one has ever tried to climb this peak and thus it is a virgin peak.

b. According to another legend, a Gaddi, tried to climb along with a herd of sheep and is believed to have been turned into stone along with his sheep. The series of minor peaks around the principal peak are believed to be the remnants of the shepherd and his sheep.

c. There is yet another legend, according to which a snake also attempted to climb this peak but failed and was turned into stone.

d. It is also believed that the devotees can have a view of the Kailash peak, only if the Lord is pleased. Bad weather, when the peak is hidden behind clouds, is a sign of the Lord's displeasure.

Pilgrimage/Trekking Season

The season when the route is open for pilgrims is from June to October. The annual Manimahesh Yatra is undertaken in August-September from Chamba/Bharmour. In the month of Bhadon, on the eighth day of the new moon period, a fair is held in the precincts of the lake that attracts thousands of pilgrims, who assemble here to take a dip in the holy water.

There are two trekking routes to the lake. One is from Hadsar village that is mostly frequented by pilgrims and trekkers. The road is motorable up to Hadsar, 21 kms from

Bharmour. The last 14 kms is a strenuous trek with many boulders on the path. The other route, taken by the villagers, is from the village Holi, with a steep climb, followed by a descent to the lake. There is no habitation on this route, except for a small village.

Manimahesh Lake with camp tents on the shores

Located about 2 kms short of Manimahesh lake, are two religiously important water bodies, called Gauri Kund and Shiva Krotri. As per popular belief, Gauri and Shiva, have their bath in these two respectively. The women pilgrims take a holy dip in Gauri Kund and the men pilgrims in Shiva Krotri, before proceeding to Manimahesh lake.

At one corner of the Manimahesh lake, there is a marble image of Shiva which is worshipped by the pilgrims who visit this place. After bathing in the holy waters, the pilgrims go around the circumference of the lake three times. The lake and its surroundings, present a majestic view. The quiet waters of the lake carry the reflection of snow – capped peaks that tower over the valley.

Mountaineering

Manimahesh Kailash has not been successfully summitted by mountaineers and thus remains a virgin peak. An attempt to climb the peak made in 1968, by an Indo–Japanese team led by Nandini Patel, was aborted. It is said that no one could climb this sacred peak because it is said to be the abode of Lord Shiva and climbing it would be sacrilege, due to its inherent divinity.

CHAPTER 14

Conclusion

Whether it is a pilgrimage or hiker's trek, Kailash – Manasarovar trip is not advisable to be undertaken on an individual basis, since it involves many days of journey by landcruisers through inhospitable rough terrain and trekking through high altitude, mountainous and hazardous areas. An individual or a group has to book the pilgrimage/ trek through a registered private travel agency. The agencies will take care of all the administrative and logistic supports required such as – arranging visa, permits and foreign exchange, booking of landcruisers/minibus, guesthouse accommodation for overnight stay, porters/Sherpas for luggage movement, catering of food, a mandatory Tibetan guide to accompany the group etc. There are plenty of such agencies in India, Nepal and Tibet to choose from.

Through MEA via Nathu La the duration of pilgrimage is 22 days and via Lipu Lekh it is 26 days as 4 to 5 days are required to finish formalities vis-à-vis administrative and logistic procedures and mandatory medical check-ups. Through private travel agencies via Nepal/ Lhasa it is 16 days and via Nepalgunj and helicopter it is 9 days. The approximate cost would vary between 1.5 lakh (INR) through MEA and 2.5 to 3.0 lakh through private agencies.

The most important aspect to be considered is the physical fitness of the pilgrim to undertake this arduous task through high altitude regions where the atmosphere is rarefied, making the trek even more exhausting. Carrying of adequate medical supplies and woollens for the duration is also quite vital. All these aspects are particularly more stringent for those senior citizens who are over 70 years old.

Glossary

1. Aashiqi Park – Park near Gauri Kund on way to Kinnaur Kailash, believed to be meeting point of Lord Shiva and Parvati

2. Adhya Shakti – Female or negative energy

3. Adi Kailash – Also called Adh/Half/Little/Chhota/Shiva/Baba Kailash, a sacred peak in Uttarakhand

4. Airawat – White elephant, obtained during churning of Manasarovar, Lord Indra's mount

5. Alex McKay – Research scholar of Indo-Tibetan history

6. Angkor Wat – Temple complex in Cambodia

7. Ashrama – Dwelling for monks

8. Ashtapada – Literally eight steps signifying the eight mounts at Kailash, around the place of Nirvana/Moksha of Rishabhadeva or Adinath

9. Ashwath Vruksha – Sacred banyan tree in Hinduism

10. Atma Linga – Sacred spot in inner Kora

11. AUM/OM – Sacred symbol of Hinduism and Jainism

12. Axis Mundi – Centre or navel of the universe

13. Bagdogra – Airport in West Bengal to reach Gangtok in Sikkim

14. Bhadon – Month in August-September in Hindu calendar

15. Bharmour – Sub-division of Chamba district

16. Bheem Dwar – Camp on trek to Shikhar Kailash

17. Bheem Tal – Intermediate point to Shikhar Kailash

18   Bhode-Kosi River – Border river between Nepal and Tibet

19   Bon – Indigenous religion of Tibet

20   Bonpo – Follower of Bon religion

21   Brahma – One of the Hindu Trinity, responsible for creation

22   Brahma Kamal – Sacred flower found in hills/mountains

23   Brahma Parvat – Peak near Adi Kailash

24   Brahmaputra – Also called Yarlung Tsangpo in Tibetan, originating from Kailash

25   Budhil – Valley in Bharmour sub-division of Chamba district of Himachal Pradesh

26   Burang – County of Tibet where Mount Kailash is located

27   Cakrasamvara – Mount Kailash representing supreme bliss in Tibetan Buddhism

28   Chakra – Energy centre or solar plexus along the spinal cord

29   Chamba – District of Himachal Pradesh

30   Charansparsh – Sacred spot in inner Kora

31   Chaugan – Literally playfield of snow at base of Manimahesh peak

32   Chitragupta – Accountant of Yamlok

33   Chongdo – Spot after Zutul Puk from where road is motorable

34   Chorten – Monument or tomb of a saint in Tibetan Buddhism

35   Chuku/Choku – Buddhist monastery between Tarboche and Dira Puk

36   Darchen – Base camp for pilgrims to Mount Kailash

37 Demchok – Buddhist deity, meaning supreme bliss identified with Mount Kailash

38 Dharamsala – Basic accommodation for pilgrims

39 Dharchula – Town in Pithoragarh district, from where motorable road has been built for Kailash pilgrims

40 Dira Puk – Monastery where pilgrims halt after first day of Kora

41 Dolma La – Highest pass between Dira Puk and Zutul Puk

42 Draupadi – Wife of Pandavas

43 Ernst Muldashev Prof – Russian Doctor and explorer of Tibet

44 Frits Saal – Sanskrit and Vedic studies scholar

45 Gaddi – A hilly tribe in Manimahesh region

46 Ganesha – Son of Lord Shiva

47 Gang Rinpoche/Kang Rinpoche – Literally "Precious jewel of snow" in Tibetan

48 Ganga/Ganges – Longest holy river of India from Uttarakhand

49 Gangtok – Capital of Sikkim state, gateway to Nathu La and China

50 Garpon – A local regional leader of Tibet

51 Gauri Kund – Also called Parvati Sarovar, sacred pond where Parvati had bathed

52 Gunji – Village on Lipu Lekh route

53 Gurla Mandhata – Glacier mountain feeding Lake Manasarovar

54 Gyangzha/Gyandrak – Buddhist monastery in inner Kora

55 Gyirong – Border post on Tibetan side at bridge crossing to Nepal

56 Hadsar – Village after Bharmour from where trekking commences to Manimahesh

57 Hamsa – Swan, a mythical bird, mount (vehicle) of Lord Brahma

58 Hangrang – Valley on way to Kinnaur Kailash

59 Herbert Tichy – Austrian mountaineer, geologist and writer

60 Hilsa – Border crossing point between Nepal and Tibet near tri-junction of India-Nepal-Tibet

61 Holi – Village from where trekking by village folk commences to Manimahesh

62 Hugh Ruttledge – British civil servant and mountaineer of two Everest expeditions

63 Indus – Also called Sindhu, originating from Kailash

64 Jamuna River – Name of Brahmaputra in Bangladesh

65 Jaon – Village in Kullu, starting point of trek to Shikhar Kailash

66 Jhoola Pul – Hanging bridge near Sutlej River on trek to Kinnaur Kailash

67 Jonglingkong Lake – Also called Gauri Kund, sacred lake near Adi Kailash

68 Kali Ghati – Abode of goddess Kali on way to Shikhar Kailash

69 Kali River – River separating India-Nepal border on Indo-Tibetan route

70   Kalpavruksha – Holy tree, obtained during churning of Manasarovar

71   Kamadhenu – Holy cow, obtained during churning of Manasarovar

72   Kangma – Town between Nathu La and Kailash

73   Karnali – Also called Ghaghara, this originates from Kailash and becomes tributary to Ganga/Ganges

74   Kartikeya – Son of Lord Shiva

75   Kinnaur Kailash – Also called Kinner Kailash in Kinnaur district, Himachal Pradesh, close to Indo-Tibet border

76   Kodari – Border post on Nepal side at Indo-Nepal Friendship bridge

77   Kora – Circumambulation of a venerable object by Buddhists and Bonpos

78   Kuber Kund and valley – Sacred places in inner Kora

79   Kullu – Valley in east Himachal Pradesh

80   Kunsa – Valley during trek to Shikhar Kailash

81   Kuthi Valley – Valley near Adi Kailash

82   Lam Chu Valley – Valley between Dolma La and Zutul Puk

83   Lapcha La – Pass located in Limi valley in Humla district of Nepal

84   Lazi – Town between Nathu La and Kailash

85   Lha Chu Valley – Valley between Tarboche and Dira Puk

86   Lhasa – Capital of Tibet where palace of Dalai Lama is located, before his flight to India

87   Lhatse – Town between Nathu La and Kailash

88   Limpiyadhura Pass – Pass at Indo-Tibet border

89   Lipu Lekh La – Pass between India and Tibet in the Himalayas

90   Literally "wellbeing or good fortune", sacred symbol in Hinduism and Jainism

91   Lohit River – Joins Brahmaputra in Arunachal Pradesh

92   Luciano Petech – Italian scholar of Himalayan history

93   Mahabodhi tree – Sacred Bodhi tree in Bodhgaya

94   Maling Khata – Intermediate point during trek to Kinnaur Kailash

95   Mandala – Map/drawing/diagram of universe in Buddhist spirituality

96   Manimahesh Kailash – Also called Chamba Kailash, in Chamba district of Himachal Pradesh

97   Manimahesh Lake – Also called Dal Lake at base of Manimahesh peak

98   Mapam Yumtso – Tibetan name for Lake Manasarovar

99   Mata Girija – Form of Parvati worshipped on Manimahesh peak

100   Maya – Queen mother of Buddha

101   Meru/Mahameru/Sumeru – Literally "Spine" or "Axis"or "Central bead of rosary", referring to Mount Kailash as spiritual centre of universe

102   Milarepa – Philosopher, saint, monk of Tibetan Buddhism

103   Mircea Eliade – Romanian religious historian

104   Moksha – Liberation or Salvation

105   Muladhara – 1st or root or base chakra at the base (coccyx) of spinal cord

106   Nain Sarovar – Literally "Eye's Lake", sacred lake on way to Shikhar Kailash

107   Nandi – Bull, mount/vehicle of Lord Shiva

108   Nandi Parvat – Sacred peak in inner Kora

109   Nathu La – Border post between India and China near Sikkim

110   Nepalgunj – Town in west Nepal

111   Ngari – Prefecture in Tibet where Mount Kailash is located

112   Nyalam – Important town between Khatmandu and Kailash

113   Nyelu songs – Songs proclaiming timeless fraternity of pilgrims, sung by Tibetan pilgrims while crossing Dolma La Pass

114   Om Parvat – Sacred peak with snow deposit pattern of AUM/OM, near Adi Kailash

115   Padmasambhava – One of the founding fathers of Tibetan Buddhism

116   Panch Kailash – Literally "Five Kailashes", a collective noun for five sacred mountain peaks in the Himalayas

117   Panchabhutas – The five great elements of nature – earth, water, fire/light, air and space

118   Pandavas – Five brothers of Mahabharat

119   Parikrama – Also called Pradakshina, circumambulation of a religious object by Hindus

120   Parvati – Consort of Lord Shiva

121   Parvati Bagh – Parvati's garden during trek to Shikhar Kailash

122   Pir Panjal – Mountain range in Himachal Pradesh where Manimahesh is located

123   Prakriti – Female or negative energy

124   Prayang – Important town between Khatmandu and Kailash

125   Purusha – Male or positive energy

126   R.C. Wilson, Col. – Mountaineer

127   Rakshas Tal – Also known as Bhairav Kund or Ravan Kund, Literally "lake of the demon/devil", salt water lake at the foot of Kailash

128   Raswagarh – Border post on Nepal side at bridge crossing to Tibet

129   Ravana – Demon king of Lanka (now Srilanka), antagonist of Ramayana

130   Reinhold Messner – Italian mountain explorer and author

131   Rishabhadeva/Adinath – First Tirthankara of Jains

132   Saga – Important town between Khatmandu and Kailash

133   Sahasrara – 7th or crown chakra at the top of head, signifying enlightenment or bliss

134   Sangla Valley – Valley on way to Kinnaur Kailash

135   Sangla Village – End point of trek to Kinnaur Kailash

136   Saptarishi – Sacred spot in inner Kora

137   Selung – Buddhist monastery in inner Kora

138   Sherthang – Town in China on Nathu La – Kailash route

139   Shikhar Kailash – Also called Shrikhand Mahadev Kailash, in Kullu, Himachal Pradesh

140   Shiva – One of the Hindu Trinity, responsible for Destruction or Transformation of creation

141 Shiva Krotri – Water body or pond before Manimahesh where male pilgrims take their holy dip while proceeding to Manimahesh

142 Shiva Shakti – Male or positive energy

143 Shivaling – Rock formation symbolizing Lord Shiva

144 Shivasthal – Sacred place after Dira Puk

145 Shongtong Bridge – Bridge near Sutlej River on trek to Kinnaur Kailash

146 Simikot – Town between Nepalgunj and Tibetan border at Hilsa

147 Singhaad – Base camp of trek to Shikhar Kailash

148 Sinla Pass – Pass near Adi Kailash

149 Sutlej/Satluj – Also called Shatadru, this originates from Kailash and is the southernmost tributary of Indus River

150 Taklakot – Town between Kailash and Nepal border at Hilsa

151 Tangling Village – Starting point of trek to Kinnaur Kailash

152 Tarboche – Starting point for Kora of Kailash

153 Thaachru – Camp on trek to Shikhar Kailash

154 Thangka – Tibetan Buddhist painting/image on cloth or silk wall hanging

155 Tilicho Lake – Highest fresh water lake in the world in Nepal

156 Tirtha – Holy pilgrimage site

157 Tonpa Shenrab – Founder of Bon religion

158 Trishala – Queen mother of Vardhamana Mahavira

159   Trishul – Trident of Lord Shiva

160   Vajrayana – Buddhist tradition of Tibetans

161   Vardhamana Mahavira – 24th Tirthankara of Jains

162   Vishnu – One of the Hindu Trinity, responsible for Preservation of creation

163   Vitruvian Man – Symbolic and mathematical exploration of the human by Leonardo da Vinci

164   X'gatse/Shigatse – Second largest city between Lhasa and Kailash in Tibet

165   Yam Dwar – Gateway to Yamlok

166   Yama – Also Yamraj, God of death in Hinduism

167   Yamantaka – Buddhist shrine in Manasarovar

168   Yamlok – World where all living beings reach after death

169   Yatra – A religious journey performed by a devotee in Hinduism and Jainism

170   Yudhishthira – Eldest of the Pandavas, ruled the kingdom over a long period after the war of Kurukshetra

171   Zhangbo – Town in Tibet on way to Kailash

172   Zhangmau – Border post on Tibetan side at Indo-Nepal Friendship bridge

Bibliography

SNELLING, JOHN : Sacred Mountain, Motilal Banarsidass, Delhi, 1983

SWARN, ANURAG : Kailash Mansarovar, Prakash Books, Delhi, 2013

GUPTA, KULBHUSHAN : Kailash Mansarovar, Notion Press, Chennai, 2019

WIKIPEDIA : Mount Kailash, en.wikipedia.org

WIKIPEDIA : Mansarovar Lake, en.wikipedia.org

WIKIPEDIA : Axis Mundi, en.wikipedia.org

www.soulwindow.com : Mansarovar Lake : Mystery and Secrets Revealed

www.linkedin.com/pulse : 8 Mysteries of Mount Kailash

www.thehindu.com : Society/History and Culture

www.timesofindia.indiatimes.com : Travels/Destinations

www.kmy.gov.in : Kailash Manasarovar Yatra

www.kmy.gov.in : Kailash Tour Packages

Travel Brochures of Agencies

WIKIPEDIA : Adi Kailash, en.wikipedia.org

WIKIPEDIA : Shrikhand Mahadev, en.wikipedia.org

WIKIPEDIA : Kinnaur Kailash, en.wikipedia.org

WIKIPEDIA : Manimahesh Kailash, en.wikipedia.org

Index

Aashiqi Park
Adhya Shakti
Adi Kailash
Airawat White
Alex McKay
Angkor Wat
Ashrama
Ashtapada
Ashwath Vruksha
Atma Linga
AUM/OM
Axis Mundi

Bagdogra
Bhadon
Bharmour
Bheem Dwar
Bheem Tal
Bhode-Kosi River
Bon
Bonpo
Brahma
Brahma Kamal
Brahma Parvat
Brahmaputra
Budhil
Burang

Cakrasamvara
Chakra

Chamba
Charansparsh
Chaugan
Chitragupta
Chongdo
Chorten
Chuku/Choku

Darchen
Demchok
Dharamsala
Dharchula
Dira Puk
Dolma La
Draupadi

Ernst Muldashev Prof

Frits Saal

Gaddi
Ganesha
Gang Rinpoche/Kang
    Rinpoche
Ganga/Ganges
Gangtok
Garpon
Gauri Kund
Gunji
Gurla Mandhata
Gyangzha/Gyandrak

Gyirong

Hadsar
Hamsa
Hangrang
Herbert Tichy
Hilsa
Holi
Hugh Ruttledge

Indus

Jamuna River
Jaon
Jhoola Pul
Jonglingkong Lake

Kali Ghati
Kali River
Kalpavruksha
Kamadhenu
Kangma
Karnali
Kartikeya
Kinnaur Kailash
Kodari
Kora
Kuber Kund and valley
Kullu
Kunsa
Kuthi Valley

Lam Chu Valley
Lapcha La
Lazi

Lha Chu Valley
Lhasa
Lhatse
Limpiyadhura Pass
Lipu Lekh La
Literally "wellbeing or good
fortune"
Lohit River
Luciano Petech

Mahabodhi tree
Maling Khata
Mandala
Manimahesh Kailash
Manimahesh Lake
Mapam Yumtso
Mata Girija
Maya
Meru/Mahameru/Sumeru
Milarepa
Mircea Eliade
Moksha
Muladhara

Nain Sarovar
Nandi
Nandi Parvat
Nathu La
Nepalgunj
Ngari
Nyalam
Nyelu songs

Om Parvat

Padmasambhava
Panch Kailash
Panchabhutas
Pandavas
Parikrama
Parvati
Parvati Bagh
Pir Panjal
Prakriti
Prayang
Purusha

R.C. Wilson, Col.
Rakshas Tal
Raswagarh
Ravana
Reinhold Messner
Rishabhadeva/Adinath

Saga
Sahasrara
Sangla Valley
Sangla Village
Saptarishi
Selung
Sherthang
Shikhar Kailash
Shiva
Shiva Krotri
Shiva Shakti
Shivaling
Shivasthal

Shongtong Bridge
Simikot
Singhaad
Sinla Pass
Sutlej/Satluj

Taklakot
Tangling Village
Tarboche
Thaachru
Thangka
Tilicho Lake
Tirtha
Tonpa Shenrab
Trishala
Trishul

Vajrayana
Vardhamana Mahavira
Vishnu
Vitruvian Man

X'gatse/Shigatse

Yam Dwar
Yama
Yamantaka
Yamlok
Yatra
Yudhishthira

Zhangbo
Zhangmau

Few Captures of this Journey

Potala Palace

Sera Monastery

Desert of Tibet

River on the Route

Lake on the Route

Yak on the Route

Landcruiser convoy in Tibet Desert

Glacier at highest point

Manasarovar Lake

Sea Gulls at Manasarovar

Gorge on Kailash Route

Rocky Formation on Kailash Route

Darchen Base Camp

Dira Puk Monastery

Dira Puk - Ready to Move to Dolma La

Sino-Nepal Friendship Bridge